Phenomenology
of Spirit

Werner Marx

Hegel's Phenomenology of Spirit

A Commentary Based on the Preface and Introduction

Translated by Peter Heath

The University of Chicago Press
Chicago and London

This book is a translation of Werner Marx's *Hegels Phänomenologie des Geistes*, published by Klostermann in 1971.

Published by arrangement with Harper & Row, Publishers, Inc.

The University of Chicago Press, Chicago 60637
The University of Chicago Press, Ltd., London

© 1975 by Harper & Row, Publishers, Inc.
All rights reserved. Published 1975
University of Chicago Press edition 1988
Printed in the United States of America

97 96 95 94 93 92 91 90 89 88   5 4 3 2 1

Library of Congress Cataloging in Publication Data

Marx, Werner.
     [Hegel's Phänomenologie des Geistes. English]
     Hegel's Phenomenology of spirit : a commentary based
on the preface and introduction / translated by Peter
Heath.—University of Chicago Press ed.
             p.   cm.
     Translation of: Hegel's Phänomenologie des Geistes.
     Reprint. Originally published: New York : Harper & Row,
     1975. Includes bibliographical references and index.
     1. Hegel, Georg Wilhelm Friedrich, 1770–1831.
Phänomenologie des Geistes. 2. Spirit. 3. Consciousness.
4. Truth. I. Heath, Peter Lauchlan, 1922–   . II. Title.
[B2929.M2813   1988]   88-10751
193—dc 19   CIP
ISBN 0-226-50923-0 (pbk.)

Contents

This book is the outcome of a series of lectures and seminars given in the Graduate Faculty of the New School for Social Research in New York and at the University of Freiburg. Dr. Ludwig Siep and Dr. Bernhard Rang were of great help to me in seeing the work through the press, and for this I should like to thank them here.

W. M.

Foreword

IN RECENT YEARS many of the old questions about the interpretation of the *Phenomenology of Spirit* have again been revived,
and new ones have been added to them. A whole series of such
questions has been provoked by the later Hegel himself. There
are utterances which give the impression of his having held his
work in only very slight esteem; in others he merely judges it
with some reserve—but at all events he never wholly rejected
it.[1] Great confusion has arisen from the fact that in the larger
Logic of 1812 he gave an account of the relation of the
Phenomenology of Spirit to the whole system which differs from
that in the revised version of the *Logic* of 1831, and that the
Philosophy of Spirit in the *Encyclopaedia of the Philosophical
Sciences,* wherein "phenomenology" constitutes a special section
of "subjective spirit," again presents an altogether different view
of the matter. The question whether the *Phenomenology* should
still be viewed as in any way a part of the completed system
was bound to arise, once the *Encyclopaedia* had appeared un-
ambiguously to settle the problem of the logical starting point by
declaring that in place of the long road of the *Phenomenology,*
the "resolve that *wills pure thought*" (*Enz.,* §78; *LH,* p. 142)[2]
is sufficient to get the logical movement under way.[3]

These wavering assertions of the later Hegel, and much else,
have constantly occasioned in Hegel scholarship a renewal of the
question whether and in what sense the Phenomenology of
Spirit is an "introduction," either as a "propaedeutic" (Gabler)

or a "genesis of cognition" (Hinrichs), or in some other way, and whether and why it has to be this under the form of a "science." Above all, Hegel scholarship has already been, and will continue to be, stirred by the question whether a system in principle absolutely self-enclosed can in any way permit of an "introduction"—which may well not belong to the system—and if so, what function it can then have, in the sense that Hegel intended, or in any sense at all.[4] Closely connected with this problem there is a further question with which contemporary Hegelian scholarship is particularly concerned: Is the *Phenomenology of Spirit* a work composed in one piece,[5] or did Hegel modify its design and arrangement even while he was writing it;[6] is the text unequivocal from beginning to end, or can we—in virtue of a quite different second approach—perceive yet another text showing through it; are we dealing here, as Rudolf Haym, Theodor Haering, and lately Otto Pöggeler have supposed, with a "palimpsest"?[7] Inquiries into the genesis of the *Phenomenology*—particularly with regard to Hegel's own personal difficulties—have pointed to discontinuities and contradictions, and in the chapter on Reason, to disproportionalities in the work.[8]

The question is often put by asking whether, in the *Phenomenology*, we are dealing throughout with a "Science of the Experience of Consciousness," *or* a "Phenomenology of Spirit," or whether either one or the other holds good for only a part of the work, or if both do so for the book as a whole (cf. below, pp. 62 ff.). The edition prepared by Hoffmeister still reprints the title page,[9] which runs: "First Part. Science of the *Experience* of Consciousness". The most recent inquiries of the Hegel Archives have confirmed, indeed, that it was retained only through an error on the bookbinder's part,[10] yet there is no dispute that the *Phenomenology*, for Hegel, was meant to be a "Science of the Experience of Consciousness."[11] It was questioned even by the older Hegelian scholars whether Hegel had adhered to this intention, or whether—as I. H. Fichte thought —the First Part had been composed from the standpoint of a transcendental philosophy, while the Second Part—as Haym saw

it—had been conceived in terms of a philosophy of history and
"*Realphilosophie.*" [12] Later Hegelian scholarship has posed this
question in similar fashion, and has mostly done so in regard to
the arrangement, and the reinterpretation of many concepts resulting from the account given of spirit. An important part is
played here by a viewpoint which earlier inquiries often neglected
to consider, namely, that behind the *Phenomenology* there may
possibly stand the Jena Logic and Metaphysics, which has now
been reliably assigned to the year 1804,[13] and would in that
case require acceptance of important changes in the sequence
of the categories.[14] In all these considerations it is naturally
of the greatest importance to determine whether and how far
the "Introduction," which was supposed to specify the "method,"
is valid for the whole work, and whether and to what extent the
"Preface" has validity for it.

The Preface has already led earlier Hegelian scholars to raise
questions about Hegel's view of the significance of "history" in
the *Phenomenology of Spirit.* Even for the young Hegel, history
played an important part, as history of the human spirit in
general, of religion, of the spirit of a people, and so on. As
world history and as history of philosophy it became, from the
Jena period onward, the topic of various lecture courses. From
thence, Hegel's view of history exerted the greatest influence on
the development of philosophy in the nineteenth century; in
particular, it had a decisive effect upon the shaping of the basic
conceptions of Marxism.

The question about the significance of history for the *Phenomenology,* and about the particular nature of its historicity,
remains a disturbing one. The peculiar historicity of the *Phenomenology of Spirit,* as displayed in the Preface, the concluding
sections of the work, and more especially in the overall movement of the development depicted therein (cf. below, pp. 28, 60),
has provoked contemporary philosophy to ask, more particularly,
in what sense the antinomy of a "history of the Absolute" is
conceivable.

The debates over most of the problems mentioned can be
regarded as contributions to the problem of the "Idea" of the

whole work. Now the latter question can be put in various ways. It can be addressed to the *Phenomenology* from the perspective of the completed system, and then becomes a matter of asking what purpose and what business the work can still actually have in the context of a self-enclosed, autonomous system.[15] The same question can also be posed out of an interest in the history of the work and its development, especially with reference to the altered view of the Jena Logic and Metaphysics necessitated by recent Hegelian scholarship;[16] and it can equally be evolved systematically from the problems of the Jena period, as the question of whether and how these problems have found expression in the matters at issue in the *Phenomenology of Spirit*.[17]

It is the intention of the present inquiry to work out the "Idea" of the *Phenomenology* by means of an interpretation expressly confined merely to the "Introduction" and "Preface" of that work. In contrast to the prevailing opinion, we take the view that the Preface largely constitutes a supplement to the Introduction, and thus was not meant to be merely a preface to the system that follows (cf. below, pp. 53 ff., 64).

This interpretation seeks to proceed only in an "immanent" fashion. In so doing we are not, indeed, of the naïve opinion that it is possible for us to interpret the text "as it stands." In the light of our present-day historical awareness, such a claim could scarcely be sustained. It is not necessary to belong to the "hermeneutic school" in order to realize that any reading of texts is governed by "prejudices" and general "presuppositions" which the reader brings to them.[18]

There is a difference, nonetheless, between an "immanent" exposition, which undertakes to interpret the *Phenomenology* without grinding any philosophical axes of its own, and an "assimilative" account. Present-day examples of such assimilation are to be seen in the endeavors to interpret the *Phenomenology of Spirit*—or usually only parts of it—from a phenomenological, ontological, Marxist, existentialist, or history-of-Being viewpoint. As was already the case with Karl Marx, the majority of these assimilations are born of the needs of the time, and seek to effect a fundamental transformation of man and reality (Lukács, Kojève, Bloch, Habermas).

Among these assimilations of the *Phenomenology* one must also distinguish, however, between two basically different types. In the first, the author himself interprets the text of the *Phenomenology* or takes up a position toward questions of its composition, etc., but does so expressly and deliberately in the light of his own general philosophical enterprise. A notable example in our own day is Heidegger's attempt to interpret the "Introduction" to the *Phenomenology of Spirit* in terms of a history of Being.

A second type of assimilation is to be found when the author adopts the textual exposition or views about the composition of the *Phenomenology* which have been worked out by a whole particular school of Hegelian scholars (e.g., those of Rosenkranz, Haym, or Haering), where this is done simply in order to support or elucidate his own philosophical enterprise. The important thing is that in this case the author foregoes either interpreting the text on his own account or adopting any attitude to problems immanent in the work.

The first type of assimilation, in which the *Phenomenology* is interpreted "productively"—by changing it—is certainly the most important philosophically; but the second is also perfectly legitimate. The latter is questionable only if it takes over a fixed view of Hegel, without ascertaining whether it is still tenable, given the state of Hegelian studies at the time. It must be insisted with emphasis that some views of Hegel may simply be misunderstood. To prevent such misunderstandings is an important task of the immanent type of interpretation. This is urgent in our own day, precisely because of the numerous and varied attempts (already mentioned) at assimilations of the second type. And such an interpretation should be able to measure up to the task particularly effectively today, now that a movement in contemporary philosophy has for the first time taken as its theme the understanding of "meaning," and has defined anew the nature and aim of hermeneutics. A hermeneutically oriented "immanent" interpretation will inquire into the "meaning" or the "Idea" of a work, such as the *Phenomenology of Spirit*, and will seek a unitary dimension from which the intelligibility of the whole work can be demonstrated. The dimension that gives unity can be sought in a leading problem which has found in Hegel its final or rather preliminary solution, or else—as will be the outcome of our own inquiry—it can be seen in the principle of a philosophical epoch which attained fulfillment in Hegel's work. At all events, it is thereby possible, on the one hand, to gather the wealth of individual problems in the *Phenomenology*, as they present themselves to the Hegel interpreter, into a single question which lends a heightened relevance to the whole. On the other hand, for attempts at assimilation, at least of the second sort, a fully worked-out Idea of the *Phenomenology* should serve as a standard which ought not to be treated with neglect.

NOTES

1. Cf., for example, *Encyclopaedia of the Philosophical Sciences*, §415a (*Hegel's Philosophy of Mind*, tr. W. Wallace and A. V. Miller, p. 156), in which Hegel gives a disparaging estimate of the Kantian philosophy as "containing the propositions only of a *phenomenology* (not of a *philosophy*) of mind." Cf. also Hegel's letter to Schelling (*Briefe von und an Hegel*, ed. J. Hoffmeister, vol. 1, Hamburg 1952, pp. 161 f.), where he talks of an "unfortunate confusion," a "greater deformity" of the later parts of the work, which is excused on the ground that he "finished the editing around midnight before the Battle of Jena" (cited from Walter Kaufmann, *Hegel*, Garden City, N.Y. 1965, p. 319). For assessment of the *Phenomenology of Spirit* on the part of Hegel's students, cf. O. Pöggeler, "Zur Deutung der *Phänomenologie des Geistes*," pp. 257 ff., in *Hegel-Studien*, vol. 1, Bonn 1961, pp. 255–94.

2. Quotations from Hegel's works are given as follows: *Phänomenologie des Geistes*, ed. J. Hoffmeister, Hamburg 1952 (English translation: *The Phenomenology of Mind*, by J. B. Baillie, 2nd ed., London 1949). Cited as *PG* and *PM* respectively.

Preface (*P*) and Introduction (*I*) are cited by paragraph in the German, and by page number from Baillie's translation respectively; the deficiencies of this work have also made it advisable, however, to cite occasional passages from the Preface in the version by Kaufmann (*op. cit.*, pp. 363–459), and from the Introduction in that by Kenley Royce Dove, in Martin Heidegger, *Hegel's Concept of Experience*, New York 1970, pp. 7–26 (cited as *K* and *D* respectively). These will be found in the notes.

Wissenschaft der Logik, vols. 1 and 2, ed. G. Lasson, Leipzig 1934 (English translation: *Hegel's Science of Logic*, by A. V. Miller, London 1969). Cited as *WL* and *HSL* respectively.

Enzyklopädie der philosophischen Wissenschaften im Grundrisse (1830), ed. F. Nicolin and O. Pöggeler, Hamburg 1959 (English translations: vol. I, *The Logic of Hegel*, by W. Wallace, 2nd ed., Oxford 1892; vol. II, *Hegel's Philosophy of Nature*, by A. V. Miller, Oxford 1970; vol. III, *Hegel's Philosophy of Mind*, by W. Wallace and A. V. Miller, Oxford 1971). Cited as *Enz*, *LH*, *HPN*, and *HPM* respectively.

Unless otherwise stated, all other works are cited from G. W. F. Hegel's *Werke*, complete ed. by a group of friends of the deceased, 17 vols., Berlin, 1832–45 (*Werke*).

Kant, Fichte, and Schelling are cited from the following editions: Kant, *Critique of Pure Reason*, tr. Norman Kemp Smith, London 1929.

Fichte, *Sämtliche Werke*, ed. I. H. Fichte, Berlin 1845–46.

Schelling, *Sämtliche Werke*, ed. K. F. A. Schelling, Stuttgart 1856–61.

3. Cf. *WL* I, 8 (*HSL*, p. 28). Compare the revised Logic of 1831: *Wissenschaft der Logik*, ed. G. Lasson, I, p. 54. And see also §36 of the Heidelberg Encyclopaedia, in *Sämtliche Werke*, ed. H. Glockner, vol. 6, Stuttgart 1938, pp. 48–49. On the problem of "reinterpreting the *Phenomenology*," cf. Hans Friedrich Fulda, *Das Problem einer Einleitung in Hegels Wissenschaft der Logik*, Frankfurt 1965, pp. 105 f. On the very diverse appraisals of the *Phenomenology* in regard to the system, on the part of Hegel's disciples and the older Hegelian scholars, cf. *ibid.*, pp. 57 ff., and especially the very useful survey on pp. 77 f.

4. Among recent writers, cf. especially H. F. Fulda, *op. cit.*, who sums up on pp. 110 f., and O. Pöggeler, *op. cit.*, pp. 259 ff.

5. This is what H. F. Fulda, *op. cit.*, attempts to show; for criticism, see O. Pöggeler, "Die Komposition der *Phänomenologie des Geistes*," pp. 52 ff., in *Hegel-Studien*, Supplement 3, Bonn 1966, pp. 27–74.

6. On the problem of arrangement, cf. Th. Haering: "Die Entstehungsgeschichte der *Phänomenologie des Geistes*," in *Verhandlungen des 3. Hegel-Kongresses*, ed. B. Wigersma, Tübingen-Haarlem 1934, pp.

118–38; and compare O. Pöggeler, "Zur Deutung . . . ," *op. cit.*, pp. 280, 289, and the same author's "Die Komposition . . . ," *op. cit.*, pp. 31, 50.

7. So R. Haym, *Hegel und seine Zeit. Vorlesungen über Entstehung und Entwicklung, Wesen und Werth der Hegel'schen Philosophie*, Berlin 1857, p. 238. Likewise Th. Haering, *op. cit.*, pp. 119 f., 133. The same view has lately been upheld by O. Pöggeler, "Zur Deutung . . . ," *op. cit.*, pp. 264 ff., and "Die Komposition . . . ," *op. cit.*, p. 48.

8. For the problem of the chapter on Reason, cf. especially O. Pöggeler, "Zur Deutung . . . ," *op. cit.*, pp. 272, 278, and "Die Komposition . . . ," *op. cit.*, pp. 47, 49 f.

9. The question of the title was first raised by C. F. Bachmann, *Anti-Hegel*, Jena 1835, p. 182. Cf. O. Pöggeler, "Zur Deutung . . . ," *op. cit.*, pp. 262 ff., 271 ff.

10. So O. Pöggeler, "Zur Deutung . . . ," *op. cit.*, p. 272, and "Die Komposition . . . ," *op. cit.*, p. 31.

11. Cf. again O. Pöggeler, "Zur Deutung . . . ," *op. cit.*, p. 272.

12. The name "Phenomenology" first appeared in the Lecture Prospectus of 1806–7; cf. O. Pöggeler, "Zur Deutung . . . ," *op. cit.*, p. 288; on the controversy, cf. *ibid.*, pp. 267 ff.

13. On the interpretation of the 1804 Logic, cf. O. Pöggeler, "Die Komposition . . . ," *op. cit.*, pp. 95 f., and H. Kimmerle, "Zur Entwicklung des Hegelschen Denkens in Jena," in *Hegel-Studien*, Supplement 4, Bonn 1969, pp. 33 ff.

14. On this cf. O. Pöggeler, "Die Komposition . . . ," *op. cit.*, pp. 37 ff., and H. F. Fulda, "Zur Logik der Phänomenologie von 1807," pp. 95 ff., in *Hegel-Studien*, Supplement 3, Bonn 1966, pp. 75–101.

15. This is precisely the topic of the work by H. F. Fulda, *op. cit.*

16. That is the primary viewpoint of the already-cited inquiries by O. Pöggeler.

17. So R. Bubner, "Problemgeschichte und systematischer Sinn einer Phänomenologie," in *Hegel-Studien*, vol. 5, Bonn 1969, pp. 129–59.

18. On this set of problems, see Hans-Georg Gadamer, *Wahrheit und Methode*, 2nd ed., Tübingen 1965.

Historical Review

In order to characterize the position of the Hegelian metaphysics within the metaphysics of his time, and from thence to obtain a first prospect of the "Idea" of the *Phenomenology of Spirit,* let us begin by inquiring into the immediate antecedents of the *Phenomenology* in the first phase of German Idealism, i.e., in Fichte and the young Schelling. In both we find the idea of a genetic presentation of the build-up of self-consciousness in its various capacities, conceived as a "sequence of reflection," in which consciousness increasingly improves in self-discernment (cf. Fichte, I, 223; English in *Science of Knowledge,* tr. P. Heath and J. Lachs, New York 1970, pp. 199 f.). In his *Foundations of the Entire Science of Knowledge* of 1794, Fichte had developed this thought, under the title of a "pragmatic history of the human mind," as the task of a Science of Knowledge; for the realm of theoretical consciousness he had executed it in the "Deduction of Presentation" * in that work, and in his *Outline of the Special Features of the Wissenschaftslehre in Regard to the Theoretical Faculty* of 1795. Schelling had seized upon this possibility of presenting a "history of self-consciousness" in his *Essays to Explain the Idealism of the Wissenschaftslehre* of·1796–97, and in the *System of Transcendental Idealism* of 1800 he had tried to carry it out.

* *Vorstellen* is only here, in connection with Fichte, translated as "presentation." In other parts of the book it is rendered by "representation." "Presentation" is otherwise carefully reserved to translate the key Hegelian word *Darstellung.*—ED.

Both of them, Fichte and Schelling alike, construct the history of self-consciousness from its beginnings, starting with the primary logical acts which still lie beyond consciousness. There follows the genesis of theoretical cognition, starting with sensation (or in Fichte's "Deduction," with intuition) as the immediate mode of cognition. In Fichte's "Deduction of Presentation" this genesis leads by way of understanding to reason; in Schelling's *System,* by way of intuition and reflection to the "absolute act of will" with which the genesis of the practical begins.

There is no need here to rehearse the entire sequence of stages in the early systems of Fichte and Schelling. The only point to require emphasis is this: Both were concerned to show that the identity of the self's pure self-intuition underlies all the theoretical and practical (and in Schelling also the aesthetic) achievements of the self, that from it all categories and forms of intuition can be deduced, and that even the "ordinary" consciousness, which distinguishes an objective world from itself, can be explained by way of a self-limitation of its original "intellectual intuition." Both wished to show in this connection how consciousness, proceeding from an originally unconscious intuition, evolves ever-increasingly toward a reflection upon itself. Whereas Fichte was concerned in this movement only with depicting the genesis of the self, while the not-self played a subordinate part (subjective idealism), the young Schelling attempted to show that, and how, intellectual intuition is a producing of what is other to the self, namely "nature."

At the end of the road this reflection arrives, at all events, at insight into an original identity, and hence at the very same thought—though now filled, of course, with content—from which philosophical reflection first set out. Both Fichte and Schelling take the view—no less than did Hegel later on in the *Phenomenology*—that philosophical reflection "can only follow · [natural reflection], but can give it no law" (Fichte, I, 223 [Heath & Lachs, p. 199]); all that Fichte demands of the philosopher is a "perception . . . given to experiment" (*ibid.,* I, 222 [199]). In his Munich lectures on the "History of Modern Philosophy" (*Sämtliche Werke,* X, 98), Schelling describes the method of his "system" as a "Socratic dialogue" between philosophical and natural consciousness.

This idea of a history of consciousness was taken over by Hegel in the *Phenomenology,* inasmuch as the first part of that work also presents a sequence of "faculties" (sensory certainty— perception—understanding—self-consciousness); looking at the work as a whole, we find "knowledge" unfolded up to the point at which—as absolute knowledge—it arrives at insight into the identity of subject and object, and hence at a supersession of the opposition between knowing and objecthood. We do not simply start here from a self-restriction of the original intellectual intuition, but—with increasing clarity—from a restriction of "spirit," which becomes "other to itself" and alienates itself in order to find itself again in otherness, in which process the aspect of otherness, namely objectivity, will come more strongly into its own. At present this can only be hinted at (see below, pp. 54 ff.). Our point is that even before Hegel, idealism was concerned to offer a genetic account of the identity of subject and object. For a fuller explanation of the meaning of this identity, we must extend our purview beyond the immediate "antecedents" of the *Phenomenology.*

The conception of subject-object identity in German Idealism is founded upon Kant's idea of "transcendental apperception": the idea that the pure subject—conceived as a structure of fundamental logical acts—employs its synthesizing power of conception to confer logical form upon the universe confronting it. The subject is thus the origin of an a priori identity of cognition and objectivity, in the fashion which Kant defined in his "supreme principle of all synthetic a priori judgements": ". . . the conditions of the *possibility of experience* in general are likewise conditions of the *possibility of the objects of experience* . . ." (*Critique of Pure Reason,* A 158).

Hegel, at all events, saw in Kant's transcendental apperception an expression of the "Idea" of the identity of thinking and being. In his first confrontation with Kant, in the Jena essay on "Believing and Knowing," he saw, indeed, an expression of this Idea not only in transcendental apperception, but also in Kant's discovery of the "productive imagination" (*Werke,* I, *Glauben und Wissen,* 21). Imagination, for Kant—according to Hegel—is the power of determining sensibility a priori and its synthesis that of accommodating intuitions to categories, in that it produces a schema which gives meaning to the category within the intuitions; in this very fact Hegel perceived the identity in question, namely the "absolute original identity of opposites" (*ibid.*). In this and other early writings he conceived of imagination as the unconscious producing of intuitions which is "immersed" in the difference of subject and object and thereby holds them together. We may leave open the question, how far Hegel, in this passage, is reading into Kant's concept of imagination the views of Fichte, for whom imagination, as a hovering between self and not-self, is the producer of intuition. It should be noted, however, that for the later Hegel the idea of transcendental apperception takes on a greater significance than that of transcendental imagination. For in the *Science of Logic* (1812) he expressly states that the "concept" has the structure of Kant's transcendental apperception. This conviction was already basic to the *Phenomenology of Spirit;* so let us make a closer examination of this adherence on Hegel's part to Kant's transcendental apperception, and to this as the structure of the concept. Kant writes in the *Critique of Pure Reason* (B 139): "The transcendental unity of apperception is that unity through which all the manifold given in an intuition is united in a concept of the object." This means that transcendental apperception, pure subjectivity or the pure self, is what constitutes objectivity, in that it brings the manifold of intuition into the necessary connection of the concept. This necessary connection of the concept "is"—on Hegel's reading, anyway—ultimately transcendental apperception, or the self; and the particular concepts or categories under which, for Kant, the given is unified in an a priori judgment, are logical functions or modes of the self, i.e., "of" the concept. For Hegel the unifying, apperceiving activity of the self is nothing other than the "concept." He thus interprets Kant's insight into the structure of transcendental apperception as follows: the unifying oneness of the self which fulfills itself as concept is the foundation of the universal and necessary connection of objectivity. From this it follows, for Hegel, that the subject can find itself again in the other—in the realm of objectivity which it has "constituted." The very same thing will then also be part of the "Idea" of the *Phenomenology:* consciousness must abandon the idea of an objectivity independent of its knowledge and recognize that everything else is "permeated" by categories of the self, the concept—that conceiving (the concept) in its "otherness," insofar as it is "thought," remains at home with, and is identical with, itself.

In order to do justice to the meaning of the concept in Hegel, we should also not overlook, however, what separates him from Kant's understanding of the subject-object identity in transcendental apperception. To Kant pure self-consciousness in its unifying function was of importance for the possibility of synthetic judgments a priori, i.e., ultimately for supplying the basis of the empirical knowledge of natural science and its "objectivity." The problem of German Idealism, and of Hegel in particular, was more fundamental. Subjectivity, for him, was the movement which "logicizes" the whole of Being. It thereby acquires the significance which the Logos had possessed for Greek philosophy.

For the Greeks the Logos already implied an identity of thinking and Being, in that it signified both order itself and the knowledge of order. This identity betokened for them at the same time a participation of thought in the ordering of the cosmos. For modern post-Kantian philosophizing the knowing subject is the source of the order of the (categorial) objectivity of objects which takes shape in the concept. Hegel remains faithful to this "turn." The concept, for him, is the Logos expressing itself as subject, which constitutes the order and intelligibility of everything that exists. Here "subject" assuredly does not signify human, or even individual, knowing. Subject is also the order reflected in the forms and laws of nature, the ordering objective spirit of ethical life, and the "absolute spirit" which presents itself in the ordered structures of art, religion, and science. Human cognition does not produce all these orders, but traces them out comprehendingly. But because this logicization has always taken place already, knowing is not, as in Kant, a giving of form to what was previously formless, but a becoming manifest to itself of the movement of the concept, which, as Logos, rules in everything. The concept attains to a condition of being completely manifest to itself, once it has permeated everything "other" to it and "sublated" this to itself. The path of this ever-increasing self-permeation is the movement which takes place in the distinction of the knowing and knowingly acting self and its "object." The presentation of this road is, in fact, the Phenomenology of Spirit.

This is enough to make it clear that Hegel's metaphysics is part of the tradition of Logos philosophy, even though it takes over the Logos in its specifically modern version, authoritatively defined by Kant. But in this traditional sense of the Logos by which Hegel is guided, there also lie further determinations which have likewise become operative in the *Phenomenology*. The Logos, by tradition, not only signifies the identity of thinking and Being—or, in modern terms, of subjectivity and objectivity; even for the Greeks it already had the meaning of an order which—at least potentially—must be totally obvious and traceable by everyone. The Logos as thought or thinking continues to preserve this translucency. *Nous*—"spirit" or "reason" —is the light-giving principle; and thinking, as *noesis,* is the possibility granted to man for an intuitive apprehension which brings to light and is never subject to error; the realization of Logos as *dianoia*—"understanding"—occurs as a knowing which grasps, judges, infers, induces, and deduces, and is able to give definitions and determine essences. This power of *nous* and the Logos culminated, for the Greeks, in a philosophy which was understood as "ontology," as a search for the ultimate categorial determinations of the existent, and likewise for those of the highest existent, *theos,* insofar as ontology was always at the same time theology. The most important category in this onto-theological order was considered by Aristotle to be that of *ousia,* or substance, which was articulated into numerous types, especially that of *telos.* It is very important to bear this determining of *telos* particularly in mind, because the thought of an "attained goal" or of the "fulfilled purpose," which from the outset directs back everything that is to itself, was capable thereby of lending a definite kind of "necessity" both to what is individually as well as to the connection of all that is, the cosmos.

It will become apparent that Hegel's *Phenomenology* remains pledged to the Logos tradition in all the respects we have mentioned, not only in the idea that thinking and being are identical, but more especially in the belief that the power of Logos and *nous* must preserve total translucency. Hegel's conception of the nature of philosophy remains onto-theologically oriented, albeit in a form extensively altered through the history of philosophy; and the order still viewed as categorial is also critically determined in his case by the category of "substance," though this itself, to be sure, is viewed in the modern fashion as "subject," in the sense already indicated. In the category of substance, however, Hegel also sees the *telos* and the "necessity" implicit in the teleological cycle, which dominates the whole of order for him; the latter is admittedly no "cosmological" order conceived on the model of *uranos,* but rather the order of the concept unfolded into a system.

Hegel's
Phenomenology
of Spirit

I

Natural Consciousness

IT WAS emphasized in the Foreword (pp. ix ff. above), that both earlier and more recent Hegel scholarship are in agreement that the *Phenomenology of Spirit* was *intended* to be a "Science of the Experience of Consciousness," and that in its first sections it actually is so. In what follows we shall first of all attempt to determine the meaning, or "Idea," of such a science.

The first question to arise is whether, in the title "Science of the Experience of Consciousness," we are dealing with a subjective genitive—whether it points to a science which is itself carried out as an experience of consciousness. To all appearance the answer is "no." §15 of the Introduction makes a clear separation of science from consciousness, "which is in the grip of experience itself" (*PM*, p. 144).[1] There, as elsewhere in the Introduction and text of the *Phenomenology,* the scientific observer is distinguished, by the designations "we" or "us," from this experiencing process of consciousness. Moreover, science, which appears in the form of a "presentation," is described as a "relating" to its object (*I*, §9, *PM*, p. 139); there this object is termed "phenomenal knowledge" (*ibid.*). It is phenomenal knowledge therefore, and not science, which "has experiences."

Now §5 defines the exposition of "phenomenal knowledge" as the "pathway of the natural consciousness which is pressing forward to true knowledge" (*PM*, p. 135). "Phenomenal" knowledge—the object of the exposition—therefore seems to be a specific mode of "natural consciousness." So we first have to explain what is meant by "natural consciousness."

1

The term "natural" should not mislead us into assuming that we are concerned here with a determining of man in his natural state. We must resist from the beginning the erroneous idea that the *Phenomenology of Spirit* is attempting to define man in his wholeness, in the manner, say, of Feuerbach, of Marx's early writings, or even of a contemporary anthropology. This science is exclusively preoccupied with "consciousness"; but "consciousness," for Hegel, always signifies the cognitive relation of a self to objecthood. The fact that Hegel takes this view of consciousness as a matter of course has its background in the history of philosophy. "Consciousness" first came to be spoken of, in the history of modern thought, once Descartes had defined the ego as a *res cogitans,* and the modes of operation of this *res* as *cogitationes.* The peculiarity of these *cogitationes* lay in the structure of the movement whereby the *ego cogitans* (the subject), in relating itself to itself, refers itself at the same time to its opposite, the other or object (ob-ject), and on the basis of this double relation becomes certain both of itself and of the known object related to it. This Cartesian principle of self-consciousness was among the "self-evident truths" of the "culture" of Hegel's day. On a non-philosophical level it ranked as a basic feature both of a self-certain "common sense," and also of the "understanding" of the positive sciences, which strives for universal certainty in its laws. In Kant's transcendental philosophy this principle of movement took shape as the "form," the spontaneous logical act, through which the pure self engenders itself and "creates" its other, "nature," the sphere of objecthood, in the sense that the logical form of the pure self gives shape to the formless and organizes it by means of categorial syntheses. Since the movement of the pure self continually returns from its relation to the sphere of objecthood back to itself, since in this sense it represents a movement of "reflection," the philosophizing which gave expression to this transcendental pattern of movement conceived itself as a "philosophy of reflection." Its character will have to be more closely specified. For the present we have been concerned only to show why, for Hegel, the mention of "consciousness" signified at once and without further

2

ado the relation of the self-certain ego to an objecthood known as certain.

But what is the meaning of the qualification "natural," as applied to consciousness? Naturalness does not mean "bodily existence" or "organic nature." As Hegel explains more fully later on in the "anthropology" section of the *Encyclopaedia of the Philosophical Sciences (HPM*, pp. 29–152), the victory over the organic nature which dominates spirit lies precisely in this, that the increasingly awakening spirit is able to cultivate itself into "consciousness," and then on to "self-consciousness" and to "reason." For Hegel this term "nature" means simply the factor which binds and determines. This is still present, indeed, in the element of consciousness. But here it prevails as an "inorganic" nature (*P*, §28, *PM*, p. 90; cf. *PG*, pp. 210 ff., *PM*, pp. 315 ff.). This designates "the given circumstances, situation, habits, customs, religion and so forth" (*PG*, p. 225, *PM*, p. 333), i.e., all the circumstances in the total situation which consciousness inhabits and which determine it. The natural consciousness "exists" essentially in immediate unity with the total situation which at any given time dominates and determines it; it belongs thereto, although the situation may rank for it as a sphere of objecthood standing opposed to it. This immediate unity of consciousness and determining situation was referred to by Hegel in the *Phenomenology* as the "shape" of consciousness (cf. *I*, §17, *PM*, p. 144; and *PG*, p. 177, *PM*, p. 282).[2] "Natural consciousness" appears in a multitude of "shapes." This is the reason why the naturalness of consciousness is not "natural" in the sense of an "eternal" nature, but is rather, on the contrary—and just because of the changing situation—a changing, and in this sense a "historical" consciousness. This historical character of the protean consciousness is further attested by the fact that even all bygone "shapes now laid aside" (*P*, §28, *PM*, p. 89) belong to the "inorganic nature" (*ibid.*) of any given consciousness. As a historical consciousness, natural consciousness changes. The transformation of any current shape of natural consciousness into another is its education.

Education initially has the meaning of a thorough cultivation.

The forces which have cultivated the natural consciousness included "in ancient times" (*P*, §33, *PM*, p. 94) philosophy. The cultivation of the naturalness of consciousness by philosophy "canceled" its conception of an "immediate reality." It reduced reality to "abbreviations," i.e., to "simple thought-determinations" (*P*, §29, *PM*, p. 91), thereby purifying the individual from the immediate sensory mode of his "knowing," and transforming the "content" of his knowing into a "thought" (*ibid.*). The totality of what is thought, of thought-determinations, is called by Hegel in accord with the modern tradition "substance," although it must be noted at the same time that he often also employs this term in a wider and not strictly categorial sense. Through cultivation, this substance has become the "property" of the self; it has come to belong to the "self"—though still in an immediate fashion. This example for the historical character of the "natural" consciousness shows at the same time how its further education lies in cultivation. Further education means that the individual "assimilates his inorganic nature into himself and takes possession of it for himself" (*P*, §28, *PM*, p. 90). Consciousness sloughs off the naturalness determining it, until the latter has been wholly "assimilated." Consciousness, for Hegel, must in no case remain "natural" in the sense of having to remain dominated by quite specific circumstances of a total situation. On the contrary, further education leads increasingly to a liberation from such bondage. But what sort of liberation is intended here, seeing that Hegel has simultaneously described the assimilation as a "taking possession for himself"? The assimilation cannot be intended to mean a mere "destruction" of naturalness, of such a kind that, at the end of its course of education, consciousness has "abstracted" from all the contents determining it and reverted back to its pure self, nor can it mean that in practical action it has accommodated the sphere of objecthood to the pure self or to reason. Fichte, say, might have been able in this sense to envisage the assimilation as a "destruction" of the not-self. For Hegel the completed education of consciousness represents a liberation from the dominance of naturalness, in the sense that it grasps the rationality of objecthood, of objectivity—whether it be that of nature or of the institutions and thought-habits of a people or epoch—and thus becomes aware of its identity with this objectivity. Consciousness does not therefore simply negate the naturalness determining it, but recognizes that a discernible movement of thought-determinations is at the basis even of ideas, habits, customs, etc. By grasping what this total situation determining it truly is, it liberates itself from inorganic nature and sublates its determinacy by ideas which are not transparent to it. It is important to bear in mind that the liberation from bondage does not lead to a divorce of consciousness—as pure self-certainty—from objectivity, since this, in Hegel's view, would result only in an empty "arid" self. On the contrary, the whole relationship remains, and it is precisely thereby made manifest that the grasping of objectivity, as a rational matter wholly under the sway of thought, overcomes the separation of consciousness and objecthood (in the broad sense in which "total situation" was used earlier), and thereby eliminates the dependence of consciousness on the latter.

To our question about the nature of "natural consciousness" we have now obtained the following answer: as consciousness it has the movement-structure that has reached determination in modern philosophy; as a "natural" consciousness it is a shape that is in immediate unity with the total situation determining it; essentially, however, it is in process of liberating itself from this very bondage in the manner described, and hence will appear in different shapes, according to its level of "education," as a more or less "natural" consciousness. This it is wholly as an "immediate" mode of "spirit." It still has to be shown more exactly what is meant by this.

NOTES

1. ". . . engaged in the experience itself" (*D*, p. 25).
2. On the problem of "shapes," see H. Schmitz, "Der Gestaltbegriff in Hegels *Phenomenologie des Geistes* und seine geistesgeschichtliche Be-

deutung," in *Gestaltprobleme der Dichtung, Festschrift für Günther Müller*, Bonn 1957, pp. 315 ff.

In the section on Reason C (AA), and more especially in subsection A, "Observation as a function of Reason," consciousness does not invariably figure as a "shape."

On the distinction between "shapes of consciousness" and "shapes of a *world*," cf. *PG*, pp. 314–15; *PM*, pp. 459–60.

In Hegel's later philosophy there is no further mention of "shapes"; they no longer occur even in the Preface to the *Phenomenology*.

II

Phenomenal Knowledge

WE NEXT ASK what it means to say that the "natural consciousness," which is engaged in the experience, is an object of presentation as "phenomenal knowledge." The question at issue is the
identity of phenomenal knowledge and natural consciousness.
Is every knowing on the part of natural consciousness a phenomenal one, or is it a matter of a "qualified" mode of knowing
on the part of natural consciousness, and if so, which?

The question of the relationship of natural consciousness and
phenomenal knowledge has so far not received detailed discussion in the literature on Hegel. But it is decisive for an understanding of the Hegelian *Phenomenology*. An answer may be
obtained, perhaps, from §§5–8 of the Introduction, in conjunction with those indications given in the Preface which we have
already dwelt on with reference to the naturalness of natural
consciousness (cf. above, pp. 1 ff.). §5 of the Introduction
explains that the presentation of phenomenal knowledge can
be taken, from one particular standpoint, as "the pathway
of the natural consciousness which is pressing forward to true
knowledge." [1] But every act of knowing claims to be a "true"
one, i.e., to have apprehended the subject matter, the authentic
truth, as it is. So how, then, can there be any talk at all of
natural consciousness—which means the knowing consciousness—
first striving toward "true knowledge"? This makes sense only
if the description "true" knowledge is meant to characterize
a knowledge which can in no way be superseded by a "knowing

better," because it knows something in its entirety. Knowing would have to be of such a kind that it is party to a complete, and in that sense absolute, truth. §5 of the Introduction confirms that by "true" knowledge Hegel meant a knowing of this sort; for him there is a knowing which does thus stand in the realm of a complete truth, whose "ray" it is that "comes in contact with us" (*I*, §1, *PM*, p. 132).[2]

It is important for an understanding of all that follows that here, at the very outset of our discussion, we attempt to make clear what is meant by Hegel's talk of "absolute knowledge" and "absolute truth," or simply "the Absolute." This is all the more important in that even today—in the wake of Feuerbach and Marx—there is a tendency to suspect at once a "mystification" or a purely religious category in the definition of the "Absolute." It is true enough that, according to Hegel, the divine essence presented by the religious consciousness is "absolute," but where he is speaking of the knowing or conceiving of "what exists *per se*" (I, §1, *PM*, p. 131),[3] the term "absolute" has nothing to do with this religious content. The purpose of the *Phenomenology of Spirit* is to present the fact that, and how, the knowing, self-certain self can attain to such a grasp of "reality," the other, in its ultimate determinations and categories, that it again finds its own self, i.e., its formative thought-determinations, therein. This total permeation of the content, for which there is then no longer anything alien, is at once true or absolute knowing, or the absolutely true, or truth, or "the Absolute."

We shall see in more detail that one of the tasks of the *Phenomenology of Spirit*—which contributes essentially to determining its Idea—is in fact the history of the gestation of this concept of knowledge or science, as the realization of what Hegel calls the "concept." That the object, or objectivity, is ultimately rooted in the concept, as the unity of self-consciousness, transcendental apperception, or subjectivity, was first perceived by Kant. But for Kant this identity of subjectivity and objectivity did not signify the absolute cognition of an absolute truth. Such a cognition would exist, he thought, only for an *intellectus divinus*. Kant views "our" cognition, says Hegel, as a finite subjective faculty whose "nature and limits" (*I*, §1, *PM*, p. 131) it is the task of the transcendental critique to determine, precisely because the latter is able to demonstrate that this faculty is *not* able "to secure" (*ibid.*) for consciousness "what exists *per se*" (or "is in itself"). The transcendental critique is directed to the conditions of the possibility of cognition, because it has undertaken the task of examining the standards of validity of all judgment to see if they are legitimate, and it seeks to find out the "most fitting" mode of finite cognition (cf. *ibid.*), and to show that even if it cannot grasp absolute truth, it can still furnish truth "of another kind" (*I*, §3, *PM*, p. 133), by which Kant meant that of Galilean and Newtonian natural science. But in this examination of cognition, Kant—so Hegel reproves him—has let himself be guided by untested "natural ideas" about its essential nature. These natural ideas include above all the models of an instrument and a medium. At one moment Kant pictures cognition as if it involved a spontaneous manipulation with an instrument—"it is as though men could set forth upon the search for truth with spears and staves" (Hegel, *Werke* XV, 555; *Lectures on the History of Philosophy*, tr. E. S. Haldane and F. H. Simson, 1896, III, p. 428); alternatively, Kant envisions cognition as wholly receptive, as though it were a medium in which what is to be known has first to be refracted as if according to a law of optics. In both cases cognition fails to make contact purely with the "*per se*" (or "in-itself") to be known. It can only seize upon what "appears" to it as the work of its own instruments, or as something refracted through the medium of its cognition. For a knowledge of this sort, which can apprehend only "appearances" and not the "thing-in-itself," there is thus a boundary between the latter and cognition; cognition stands on the one side for it, and the Absolute on the other (*I*, §2, *PM*, p. 133).

In §1 (*PM*, p. 131) Hegel has pointed out still more exactly the error of a critical examination which views cognition—whether in the image of an instrument or a medium—as a "means": it moves in a circle. If it has devoted all its efforts to a critical determination of the scope of the instrument's shaping functions, i.e., that which cognition performs as a shaping act, then the critical determination of the function of cognition consists merely in taking these very forms away again from the "thing-in-itself," as mere subjective appendages. Alternatively, if the critical examination endeavors to find out the "law of refraction," as the mode in which what is to be known appears in cognition as the medium, then in fact it merely takes away again from the "thing-in-itself" the "law of refraction," i.e., the very thing it had previously pointed out. Hegel is convinced that with these untested models of the instrument and the medium Kant has obstructed insight into the conceptual nature of self-consciousness. Self-consciousness is the concept, the logical form, which however is not only static, like the transcendental apperception in Kant, but exhibits a historical movement, freeing itself on the one hand from all natural ideas (cf. above, pp. 3 f.), and itself able, on the other, to determine its own content. This means at the same time that self-consciousness, *qua* concept, is able to permeate in thought everything other and alien to it, as its own other, and as essentially one with itself. The power of the conceptuality of self-consciousness lies precisely in this, that it is ever-increasingly able to attain to an absolute self-certainty within itself, just as it is also able to know the other in its truth, as of the same nature as the self. Thus the final state of this self, which advances historically toward ever-greater certainty and truth, is that wherein it rediscovers itself in its ultimate determinations, the rules of its thinking, the thought-determinations in all otherness, objecthood and objectivity. This complete rediscovery of its subjectivity in all objectivity is precisely what constitutes the conceptual nature of self-consciousness, which it is able to present. The thought-determinations presented in all their completeness have the form of a "system," the system of the Science of Logic. It is that which is "absolutely true" for a cognition as "absolute knowing"; it is "the truth," the Absolute. "The scientific system of truth can alone be the true shape in which truth exists" (*P*, §5, *PM*, p. 70 [amended]).

To our question as to the meaning of Hegel's talk about the "absolutely true," "absolute truth," and the "Absolute," the answer is therefore: the presented system of the categories and thought-determinations of the "self." Thinking and cognition do not stand contrasted to this on the other side, as it were, nor is it divided off by a "boundary"; on the contrary, thinking is the accomplishing of the thought-determinations; it is—as we shall later discuss—subjectivity which, "steeping" itself (*P*, §53, *PM*, p. 112) as absolute knowing in its object, unfolds it as the thought-determinations deriving in dialectical movement from one another and proceeding to determine the whole of the internally ordered system. The Science of Logic is the "existence" of self-consciousness realizing itself as concept (cf. *PG*, pp. 556–57, *PM*, pp. 805–6). That self-consciousness can press forward to its "true existence," to absolute knowing (*I*, §18, *PM*, p. 145), is the very thing demonstrated by the mode of presentation constituting the Phenomenology of Spirit. Its pathway is none other than that through which self-consciousness becomes absolute knowledge and as such is able to know the absolutely true. The depiction of this route is Hegel's "demonstration," which—unlike Kant's transcendental critique—does not merely revert to the faculty of the subject and define the latter "statically," but exhibits the unfolding of the concept as the power which, *qua* subjectivity, is able to permeate all objectivity. But if absolute knowing is indeed the "goal" of the experiential route of consciousness, it follows that phenomenal knowing is not in fact beyond supersession; it is relative, rather, since it does not rediscover itself completely in all categories, but always apprehends the merely determinate, and hence must succumb to error. It is a knowing which by nature keeps coming to see that it has not apprehended the *realitas*. "Natural consciousness will prove itself to be . . . not real knowledge" (*I*, §6, *PM*, p. 135). This holds for the consciousness which first finds itself on the road to becoming absolute knowledge. It is accordingly also typified by the fact that it is able to have a conscious insight into its own untruth. Hence it is also called "untrue knowledge" or "inauthentic cognition." As we shall see, its constant "having gone astray" has indeed much to do with the fact that it must run through a history of "experiences." In this respect "phe-

11

nomenal knowledge" in no way differs from the modes of knowing of the natural consciousness itself.

It is possible to suppose, however, that in another respect phenomenal knowledge is a "qualified" form of natural consciousness. One respect in which phenomenal knowledge is qualified obviously lies in the fact that, insofar as it is an object of presentation, it "presses on" as such, along the road presented, to the goal of becoming a true, absolute knowing. Do we wish to maintain by this that natural consciousness as such is not driven by any urge? The Introduction expressly emphasizes that the restlessness of thought disturbs the indolence of natural consciousness (*I*, §8, *PM*, p. 138). It must constantly "move on" beyond what is known at any given time, namely that which is known as "individual" and thus as "limited"—"and since this latter belongs to it, [beyond] its own self." Hence it must destroy its every "limited satisfaction." It may indeed be anxious at the loss of what was then known to be true, and accordingly at any "new" truth, and hence also try either to remain in "unthinking indolence," or sentimentally to persist in its assurance that a thing is "good in its kind"; or out of "vanity" it may defend its current standpoint with "zeal," and thereby gloat upon its own understanding, only to find in the process its own "barren ego" merely, instead of "all the content." But in so doing it remains constantly driven by an urge, and that because—as will soon appear in greater detail—the reason which holds sway in the "self" of natural self-consciousness, namely the "concept," inflicts this "violence" on it.

Now the natural consciousness may indeed be "driven" entirely in this fashion, but that does not yet mean that it is driven to embark on that quite specific course at whose end it becomes a true, absolute knowing; in the possibility of a historical change in the naturalness of consciousness we have, indeed, already been shown its ability to transcend a given constraint, a particular shape. But this power of releasing itself from constraints does nothing, as yet, to open up the road to self-emancipation from all constraints and presuppositions, the pathway to absolute knowing. It may be asked: Does conscious-

12

ness spontaneously seize this opportunity of becoming "absolute"? Or does it perhaps do this only after it has become an "object" of presentation, and thereby first a "phenomenal knowing"? We cannot yet at this point say anything more precise about the "role" played by presentation as the pattern of fulfillment of this science in which the Phenomenology of Spirit consists. The peculiarity of phenomenal knowing as a cognitive mode of the natural consciousness appears, at all events, to reside in this, that as object of a presentation it presses forward to this specific goal of absolute knowing, traverses the "series of [its] shapes," and is thus "the detailed history of the . . . training of consciousness itself up to the level of science" (*I*, §6, *PM*, p. 136).[4]

That phenomenal knowledge and natural consciousness do not coincide is apparent on contemplating, not only the goal of absolute knowledge, but also the law of progress toward it. The first sentence of §7 of the Introduction runs: "The completeness of the forms of unreal consciousness will be brought about precisely through the necessity of the advance and the necessity of their connection with one another" (*PM*, p. 137).[5] The necessity of the advance from one shape of unreal consciousness to another is in this case the factor which guarantees the completeness of the forms of phenomenal knowledge. This very fact, that those forms of phenomenal knowledge, which emerge as shapes of consciousness in the course of its presentation, can be completely collected in the latter, is the basis of an essential difference between natural consciousness and phenomenal knowledge. For Hegel, indeed, as we have seen, the naturalness of natural consciousness is not an anthropological constant, but a function of the history of its education: *qua* natural, consciousness has its "inorganic nature," which, as its historical total situation, directly determines it. Like natural consciousness, phenomenal knowledge also makes its appearance in historical shapes. But the historicity which characterizes natural consciousness, insofar as it is an object of presentation, and thus phenomenal knowledge, is different from that which attaches to it outside such a presentation. Outside such a presentation, its meaning could be made intelligible neither through the category of necessity, nor through that of completeness. A history of education of natural consciousness could also have, in the words of the concluding chapter of the *Phenomenology of Spirit,* the "form of free fortuitous happening" (*PG,* p. 563, *PM,* p. 806). The form of necessity, on the other hand—and this is the basic idea of §7 of the Introduction—attaches only to a kind of happening whose law of motion is determinate negation. It is that "by which"—as is said in the last sentence of §7—"the progress through the complete succession of forms comes about of itself" (*PM,* p. 137).[6] What is required, therefore, in Hegel's view, for the "detailed," i.e., completely executed, "history of the process of training and educating consciousness itself up to the level of science" (*PM,* p. 136), is a twofold condition. On the one hand it is the completeness of the forms, and on the other, that which makes this possible: the necessity of the transition from one form of knowing to another. What a history of the education of consciousness means in this connection has yet to be discussed (cf. below, pp. 28 ff., 60 ff.). It may suffice at this point to conceive the presentation of phenomenal knowledge, unlike a history of natural consciousness, as a qualified mode of historical presentation: qualified by a law of motion which is responsible for the necessity of the progress to absolute knowing and the completeness of the situations presented along the pathway.

Hence we have so far learned this about "phenomenal knowledge": It is in the first place a qualified form of natural consciousness, insofar as it alone can be said to be "pressing forward to its true form of existence" (*I,* §17, *PM,* p. 145). And thus also as it alone can be described as a "path of the soul, which is traversing the series of its own forms of embodiment, like stages appointed for it by its own nature, that it may possess the clearness of spiritual life when, through the *complete* experience of its own self, it arrives at the knowledge of what it is in itself" (*I,* §5, *PM,* p. 135, my italics).[7] But we do not yet know

1. Just what the essence of phenomenal knowledge consists in, whereby it is actually able to do this.

2. Nor have we explained how it can do this, i.e., what its own method consists in; of which all we know—from the first title of the *Phenomenology of Spirit*—is that it takes place as an "experience."

3. Nor do we know why—as is obviously Hegel's view—the natural consciousness "ought" actually to tread this path of a "phenomenal knowledge," and why this has to happen right now; in other words, why a presentation of phenomenal knowledge—as the Preface expressly claims—is "due" (*P*, §5; *PM*, p. 70) at this moment.

In order to obtain a better orientation for all that is to follow, we shall first answer the third question in the next section. This will already serve to provide indications for the other two as well.

1. *The Need for Philosophy*

Why *should* the natural consciousness take this path at all, the path taken by presentation, and whose object is "phenomenal knowledge"? And why should it take this path *now*? Why is this presentation "due"? The answer to this question is plain: this is what is necessary in order to complete the educational history of natural consciousness. To make this answer apparent, we must first explain at what stage of cultivation the natural consciousness was when presentation was undertaken. This should tell us why further education of the natural consciousness seemed necessary, and in this particular direction, toward the shape of absolute knowledge. It should also emerge from this why presentation can make this further education possible, or even claim to achieve it, and why it can do this *now*.

We shall begin by discussing this question in the light of the indications given in the Preface. The question of how the latter is related to the *Phenomenology* as a whole must be postponed until later. For in order to establish it adequately it is essential to determine whether the Phenomenology of Spirit can simultaneously be, in one and the same respect, a Science of the Experience of Consciousness (cf. below, pp. 62 ff.). In the present connection, the only point of interest is that the Preface which

Hegel wrote afterward does not cast doubt on the Introduction, but materially reinforces it.

Apart from the Preface, we shall also try to answer our question by drawing upon Hegel's observations in the journal articles of the Jena period (cf. above, pp. xix f.).

Hegel is definitely of the opinion that his epoch is "a birth time, and a period of transition" (P, §11, PM, p. 75), that a "qualitative leap" has taken place, and thus a "sunrise, which, in a flash and at a single stroke, brings to view the form and structure of the new world" (ibid.).[7a] But now this "beginning of the new spirit is the outcome of a widespread revolution in manifold forms of spiritual culture; it is the reward which comes after a chequered and devious course of development, and after much struggle and effort" (P, §12, PM, p. 76). In the previous chapter we referred briefly to the Preface's allusions to the educational history of natural consciousness in "ancient times"; they extend, for Hegel—at this general level—to that new "cultivation" of natural consciousness by the philosophy of Descartes. It was Descartes who established the principle of modern philosophy upon the nature of the self, or subject; or conversely, who made the self—which in his own day had become such out of the immediacy of substance only in an immediate fashion—the basic principle. This principle of the subjectivity of the subject is that of "the immediate certainty of self," which from now on it "knows it possesses in every type and phase of knowledge," in and for itself (P, §26; PM, p. 87). This is its "absolute . . . form" (ibid.). Upon its basis the self—in philosophic self-apprehension—will become aware of other forms also, which determine the contents of its representations, and are thus "something thought," determinations of thinking such as subject and object, nature, understanding and sensibility (P, §31; PM, p. 92). It was typical of the period immediately following Descartes that the natural consciousness simply adopted these "forms" as "known," without "critically" testing them (cf. ibid.). They merely constituted "fixed points from which to start and to which to return" in a process of "flitting between them" (ibid.).[7b]

16

At the next stage of this history of education the self has then defined itself as a "universal" self; this is the self of transcendental philosophy, which is directed critically upon itself as the framework of logical forms constituting objectivity. This critical analysis of logical forms or categories itself first constitutes thinking in the full sense; but the self which finds itself in the element of thinking is a "universal self." Thinking in the shape of knowing is an "action," and an action, indeed, of the "universal mind" (P, §30; PM, p. 92). This action is directed against merely "being-familiar" with the forms, and begins to "analyze them critically," to "separate," and by doing so to form itself into "Understanding," the "action of separating" (P, §32; PM, p. 93). Hegel profoundly admired this "exercise of the force of Understanding" as "the most astonishing and greatest of all powers, or rather the absolute power" (ibid.). By contrast, there is the "circle, which is self-enclosed and at rest, and, qua substance, holds its own moments . . . [the] immediate relation . . . [which] hence arouses no sense of wonderment" (ibid.). What Hegel finds "astonishing" here is not the circular closedness of the concrete, which mediates universal and particular as the real, but the fact that, through the analyzing labor of the Understanding, "the concrete fact is self-divided and turns into unreality" (ibid.).[8] The "portentous power of the negative," of which Hegel speaks in this passage, is immediately related, not to the work of world history, but to the power of abstracting the universal from the concrete, i.e., of separating our universal thought-determinations from the circumference of that circle, in and as which the concrete possesses existence: "But that an accident as such, when cut loose from its containing circumference—that what is bound and held by something else and actual only by being connected with it—should obtain an existence all its own . . . this is the portentous power of the negative; it is the energy of thought, of pure ego" (ibid.). This thought is again taken up in the paragraphs that follow: in modern philosophy, so we are there told, "an individual finds the abstract form ready made," though it must be added by way of qualification that "in straining to grasp it and make it his own, he rather strives to bring forward the inner meaning alone . . . the production of the universal is abridged, instead of the universal arising out of the manifold detail of concrete existence" (*P,* §33; *PM,* p. 94). The Understanding's capacity, for Hegel, is in general terms the analysis of a concrete whole into its abstract moments. For the "energy of thought, of pure ego" breaks up "an idea into its ultimate elements" (P, §32; *PM,* p. 92). Such ideas thereby turn out to be in no way the forms of representations hitherto accepted as familiar, but "the immediate property of the self," i.e., its thoughts, and as such "unreality" (cf. *ibid.*). In virtue of the power of Understanding, the determinate thoughts detach themselves from their concrete context as the immediacy of substance and become separate entities which now lead an independent "existence" of their own; but only now "are" they thought-determinations as such—to begin with, admittedly, merely as fixed and static determinations. In this fashion the analyzing Understanding has for the first time put the "portentous power of the negative" into action; it is this which now everywhere engenders major changes, in the field of practical "common sense" no less than in that of the sciences, but especially also in philosophy. It is precisely through the fact that the enlightened natural consciousness has increasingly learned to make better use of this power of the negative, that it has. finally also made possible the "gradual crumbling to pieces" (*P,* §11; *PM,* p. 75), the period preceding the "sunrise" of the new spirit and the "qualitative leap." Only with this leap, as a next step constituting the "sunrise of the new spirit," has the natural consciousness so fashioned its Understanding that it could thereby become "rational knowledge" (*P,* §13; *PM,* p. 77), which is to say that it has begun to recognize the power of negativity as a power belonging to the rational self, which is able to permeate the whole of substance and mediate the latter to itself.

In this power of negativity Hegel now perceives that factor whereby there devolves upon the activity of the understanding the task of reconciling the unscientific consciousness with science. As the common element in both, understanding (the intelligence which produces intelligibility) is the *possibility* of science: "Intelligibility is the form in which science is offered to everyone, and is the open road to it made plain for all. To reach rational knowledge by our intelligence is the just demand of the mind which comes to science. For intelligence, understanding, is thinking, pure activity of the self in general; and what is intelligible is something from the first familiar and common to the scientific and unscientific mind alike, *enabling* the unscientific mind to enter the domain of science" (*P*, §13; *PM*, pp. 76–77; my italics). These crucial sentences of §13 outline the function of the understanding's analyzing work in fashioning science into the common property of all. The general remarks in §32 (*PM*, pp. 92–93) about the work of the understanding are here applied to the entry of the unscientific consciousness into science, to the transition to understanding, or rational knowledge. To arrive at rational knowledge by way of the understanding is possible because the latter is "thinking, pure activity of the self in general," that which in §32 is described by Hegel as "the energy of thought, pure ego." So far as the intelligible (the understood) is the familiar, albeit not yet the known and apprehended, even the natural consciousness which has arrived at the present stage of education toward understanding also finds itself, so the passage just cited tells us, in the form of the pure I and thus in the element of the pure concept. But only if it were to make this element perspicuous to itself (in a manner yet to be explained in detail), and thereby realize the possibility of rational knowledge, could the natural consciousness develop—on the philosophical plane—into a properly understood "idealism," for which "existence and self-consciousness are the same being" (*PG*, p. 178; *PM*, p. 276).[9] Only then could it also, as the final stage of this educational development, attain to absolute truth and thus, as we have already seen, give existence through its absolute knowing to a system of knowledge, to science as such. It *could* progress to all this. But according to Hegel—and this is of the greatest importance for our particular question—there have been obstacles to this further development since the inauguration of the new spirit. And these must now be overcome by great effort and labor. Hegel felt himself called to this work.

In the Jena period, as appears with particular clarity in his first publication, *The Difference between the Systems of Fichte and Schelling,* his endeavors were wholly and solely directed to the aim of fighting against these obstacles and guiding the consciousness of his time in the quite specific direction which he perceived in the reason dwelling in self-consciousness; and this same goal was then later served, albeit in a different fashion, by the "presentation of phenomenal knowledge" to be executed as a Phenomenology of Spirit. In his journal articles Hegel had subjected the culture of his time to a severe "critique" (cf. *Kritisches Journal der Philosophie,* ed. by Schelling and Hegel, Tübingen 1802–3), in order thereby to awaken the merely understanding self-consciousness to the reason dwelling within it. He saw the threat and the hindrance to this development above all in those philosophical positions which made use of the power of self-consciousness only in an understanding fashion, which, without immersing themselves in the matter itself, applied their understanding thought only to already-given ideas of contents and their forms, erecting them into precise and rigid "oppositions" and "dichotomies." He saw examples of such dichotomizing contrasts of the understanding in the traditional oppositions of spirit and matter, soul and body, faith and understanding, freedom and necessity, which in the course of the progress of contemporary philosophy had taken on the form of "reason and sensibility, intelligence and nature," or—as is said in the *Differenzschrift* (*Werke,* I, p. 174)— "of absolute subjectivity and absolute objectivity." These two sides were regarded as fixed points, which could therefore never be traced back to a genuine unity. The oppositions were reinforced above all by the fact that what pertained to them was subsumed under these fixed determinations; yet it could be said of this subsumption that the separation into opposites always included also a relating, and to that extent a unification. But it was thereby possible only to create fixed and finite "totalities" (cf. *ibid.,* p. 172), whose only result was in many respects to split man's cultural "life" asunder. From this very state of sundering, the real task of philosophy has emerged. "If the power of unification disappears from man's life, and opposites have lost their living relation and interaction and are gaining independence, the need for philosophy arises" (*ibid.*, p. 174).

We do not require to enter here into the particular mode and manner in which Hegel attempted, during the Jena period, to meet this "need" by his "critique," and did so by trying to transform the false, merely "understanding" reflection into a "rational and speculative" one.[10] What matters for us is that it was this state of cultivation of the natural consciousness, determined at the "outset of the new spirit" by the reflection-philosophies, which was solely responsible for inducing him to write the *Phenomenology of Spirit,* and to undertake the "presentation of phenomenal knowledge." He must therefore have hoped for it that it would motivate the natural consciousness of his day to take the path which would transform it into an absolute knowledge, which could then give existence to the scientific system, to science. For Hegel the time was "due" for the natural consciousness to become a "scientific" one. And this actually meant for him that the philosophy of his time, above all, should "raise itself to the level" of science (*P,* §5; *PM,* p. 71). "To help to bring philosophy nearer to the form of science—that goal where it can lay aside the name of *love* of knowledge and be actual *knowledge*—that is what I have set before me" (*ibid.; PM,* p. 70). That it was also a matter of conducting the natural consciousness as such to this goal, emerges from the particular manner in which this presentation—the *Phenomenology of Spirit*—seeks to be a "preparation," and that precisely for the "unscientific" as such (*P,* §§13 and 28; *PM,* pp. 76–77, 89–90). Before acquainting ourselves more closely with this particular mode of presentation, let us cling to this much for the purpose which guides us, and to answer the question we posed at the outset: the natural consciousness ought to take the path to the determined goal, and ought to take it now, and is thus, *qua* phenomenal knowledge, to become the object of presentation, because according to Hegel this is just what was necessary to complete the course of its education. However—as we shall soon see—this is not simply to give a descriptive "presentation" of the course of education, as has been done in the brief accounts in the Preface, with reference to the educational history of the past and of Hegel's own day. The "presentation" must satisfy entirely different requirements, which likewise implies that its object, phenomenal knowledge, must also conform to them.

2. Conditions for the Presentation of Phenomenal Knowledge

The natural consciousness stands in the course of its education at a stage characterized by that principle of modern philosophy which—as already mentioned—was first enunciated by Descartes. In Hegel's view, as we saw, the beginning of a new epoch has now been reached, in which this principle can be fully carried out. This would be the case—to state it in purely formal fashion at first—if self-consciousness in the sense already indicated, as absolute knowledge, were to take up the task of presenting absolute truth as a scientific system. But this development has been hampered by the philosophies contemporary with Hegel, and by the whole culture they have determined. As we have stated, the so-called "reflection-philosophies," by a merely understandingly pursued dividing and relating, and the setting-up of fixed antitheses of the Understanding, have created profound divisions in spiritual life. If these obstacles are to be overcome, and philosophy led to the true concept of knowledge and its presentation, the contemporary natural consciousness, which is not yet "scientific" in the sense of the system in prospect, must be convinced of the fact that science alone is capable of bringing the principle of self-consciousness—on which the unscientific consciousness is also already dependent—to fulfillment in a manner appropriate to the subject. How does this have to come about? It is not done by simply "projecting" the further development of the natural consciousness to science. Such a projection, which would amount to a "propaedeutic," would have little persuasive power. It would not be a suitable "preparation." It would remain merely a "chance" affair (cf. *P*, §34; *PM*, p. 95). It would propound its standpoint as the only "true" one only in a certain way and from outside; it would merely "give assurance" of it. "*One* barren assurance, however, is of just as much value as another" (*I*, §4; *PM*, p. 135). If this presentation is also to convince the philosophizing of the present day, and move it to acknowledge the concept of science—as Hegel understands it—then it must itself already have a "scientific" character, in the sense that "the road, which leads to the notion of knowledge, becomes . . . a necessary and complete evolving process" (*P*, §34; *PM*, p. 95). Even if the presentation, as the road to science, is still not yet the thing itself, it must nevertheless already bear such a "necessity" as will have to be acknowledged by the philosophy of Hegel's day. But what must be the content of this presentation, if it is not to remain a merely external propaedeutic? It must make it its business to examine and test all the forms of knowledge which lay claim to being able to grasp the truth of the matter. Science must test the "reality" of the knowing which the various positions claim to possess. It must take issue with them critically. In his early work of 1802, "Über das Wesen der philosophischen Kritik überhaupt und ihr Verhältnis zum gegenwärtigen Zustand des Philosophierens im besonderen," Hegel had already expressed his conviction that such a critique of the various philosophical positions is possible, since "philosophy is, and can only be, but one thing," because "reason is but one" (*Werke*, XVI, p. 34). A critique of reason is therefore possible, because for this *one* reason there can also be only *one* "concept of science," and because this latter must necessarily emerge, indeed, from the principle of a self-consciousness evolved into reason.

But now a critical confrontation would still fail to convince the philosophy of the day, and so fail also to lead to an overcoming of the prevailing division, if it were content to apply this concept of science, as a critical standard, in a merely external fashion to the positions under review. Science cannot "simply reject a form of knowledge . . . as a common view of things, and then assure us that itself is an entirely different kind of knowledge" and that the aforesaid knowledge, for it, is "of no account at all" (cf. *I*, §4; *PM*, p. 134). Nor can it be done by appealing to "presages of a better" in these other modes of

23

knowing (*ibid.*).[11] For what would prevent these other positions from declaring that, for their part, "science is nothing" (*ibid.*)? Nor, on the other hand, could those other positions be convinced of the fact that their knowing is not veritable, if the critique were to content itself with pointing out that in this untrue knowledge the true is already present. For this would amount to an acknowledgment of the untrue knowledge (cf. *ibid.; PM*, p. 135).

In what manner, then, should this critique be so presented that the understanding, "unscientific" consciousness may really be convinced that it must progress to that concept of science which for Hegel constitutes the fulfillment of the principle of self-consciousness? What demands would have to be made of such a critique? The requirements are

1. It should observe the express intention of being only a "prepparation" and "introduction" for the scientific system which is due and bound to "make its appearance"; it must expressly confess for its own part that it does not yet possess the concept of knowledge, and is not yet itself an absolute cognition of absolute truth or capable of realizing itself as such. It must expressly "externalize itself from the form of the pure [concept]" (*PG*, p. 563; *PM*, p. 806 [amended]), and take as its task to "engender" as a result (cf. *P*, §20; *PM*, p. 82) the "simple concept" of science as "a whole which, after running its course and laying bare all its content, returns again to itself" (*P*, §12; *PM*, p. 76) from the "configurations . . . now become moments of the whole" (*ibid.* [amended]). It is Hegel's conviction, expressly directed against the customary view of the "false," that the latter is also part of the "whole" as the "true." It is part of it in the process which has the whole as its result (cf. *P*, §§20 and 38 f.; *PM*, pp. 82 and 97 f.). Hegel called such a process of becoming an "appearance"; to what extent he meant by this an appearance of the absolute and later of the spirit, need not be discussed at present (cf. below, pp. 62 ff.). From the viewpoint of "science"—as the subsequent scientific sys-

tem yet to be established—this presentation, which will first develop the concept of science as the result of a process, is an "appearance" (cf. *P*, §38; *PM*, p. 97). In this form too it is merely the *"first* part" of science (*P*, §35; *PM*, p. 95), whereby it first "comes on the scene" (*I*, §4; *PM*, p. 134). The presentation must so "come on the scene" that for its own part it first has to elevate itself to the concept of knowledge, to real knowledge. This is the first requirement that the presentation must satisfy.

2. But presentation implies presentation of an object. So this phenomenal character of the presentation must essentially relate to its object. All the modes of natural consciousness, which are essentially "unreal knowing," must so attain to presentation as to constitute a process, the "becoming" of a whole, which has a result proceeding from this becoming. The knowing that is the object of this science which emerges as "appearance" (or phenomenon) must thus itself be phenomenal in the same sense. The false shapes, in fact, belong to it essentially, for every shape becomes under examination a false one, which is superseded by a new truth; it is to that extent something that "disappears," and this constant disappearance of the false in the emergence of the new true shape is the "bacchanalian revel" of which Hegel speaks in the Preface (*P*, §47; *PM*, p. 105).

3. If this presentation of the contemporary natural consciousness at its present stage of education is to prove convincing, this phenomenal knowledge must be so presented as it would behave were it really "in the grip of experience itself" (*I*, §16; *PM*, p. 144); to be sure, an experience which contains the necessity of advancing along the whole determinate pathway to its goal, a goal that simply does not exist for the natural consciousness, which is just why it has got stuck in its development. It will be shown in what follows that the presentation of phenomenal knowledge does in fact seek to satisfy these requirements, and also how it does so.

NOTES

1. "... striving toward ..." (*D*, p. 25).

2. "... ray of light itself. ... touches us ..." (*D*, p. 9).

3. "... that which is in-itself ..." (*D*, p. 8).

4. "... the sequence of Shapes ... is the detailed history of consciousness' own education to the level of science" (*D*, p. 14).

5. "The *complete system* of the forms of unreal consciousness will present itself through the necessity of the progression and interrelatedness of the forms" (*D*, p. 15).

6. "... the progression through the complete sequence of Shapes takes place of its own accord" (*D*, p. 16).

7. "... path of the soul which is making its way through the sequence of its own transformations as through waystations prescribed to it by its very nature, that it may, by purifying itself, lift itself to the level of Spirit and attain cognizance of what it is in itself through the completed experience of its own self" (*D*, p. 13.)

7a. "This gradual crumbling which did not alter the physiognomy of the whole is interrupted by the break of day that, like lightning, all at once reveals the edifice of the new world" (K, p. 380).

7b. " ... and they are accepted as fixed points of both departure and return. They remain unmoved as one moves back and forth between them—and thus only on their surfaces" (K, p. 406).

8. "... the concrete differentiates itself and makes itself what is unactual ..." (*K*, p. 406).

9. "... self-consciousness and being are the same essence" (Tr.).

10. For Hegel's concept of "critique" in the Jena period, cf. now R. Bubner, "Problemgeschichte und systematischer Sinn ... ," *op. cit.*

11. "... the intimation of a better knowledge with that other" (*D*, p. 12).

III

Natural Consciousness and Science

WE HAVE FOUND that the natural consciousness and its modes of knowledge—as they have developed in history under the "form of contingency"—are *not* phenomenal knowledge. The latter consists only of that knowledge which, in the form of presentation, has become the object of the "preparatory" science which "comes on the scene," namely the Phenomenology of Spirit. Only such an objectified knowledge is on the road to the specific goal of becoming absolute knowledge. This preparatory science, for its own part, acquires the concept of knowledge only from the outcome of the process in which phenomenal knowledge advances to absolute knowledge; as we have seen, it too is for this very reason only a "phenomenon," just as its object is a "phenomenon" for the very reason that it is a process of becoming.

If the presentation of phenomenal knowledge by phenomenal science is to take place in such a way as to be able to convince the natural consciousness of Hegel's time that it too could take this route, then the possible modes of knowledge cannot simply be deduced; instead, this becoming must be demonstrated as a process, as the history of experiences that have been, or could be, "undergone"; a process in which the manner whereby these experiences succeed one another is sustained by a necessity, on the basis of which the determinate goal—absolute knowledge, the concept of knowledge—is bound to be reached. Such a presentation would be all the more convincing to the natural consciousness, if it could be shown of the concept of knowledge that it is based on the very same principle which any natural consciousness essentially rests upon, so that we are dealing here with a goal, a *telos*, to which every natural consciousness could make its way—if only it had the proper insight into its essential nature.

The *Phenomenology of Spirit* does indeed endeavor, in this fashion, to make the concept of knowledge—to which it must first elevate itself—intelligible to contemporary thought. It attempts to "justify" this concept (*WL, I*, p. 29; *HSL*, p. 48).

How does it provide this "justification"? It presents a history of experiences, as the natural consciousness could also have experienced them, if only it had taken this route; it shows, moreover, how a quite specific method—which we shall shortly discuss —necessarily conducts the course of experience to this goal, to absolute knowledge as the concept of knowledge. And above all it makes evident that the development is inherent in the principle of consciousness, and that every natural consciousness could thus develop toward this *telos* or goal. Unlike "science" as such, the Phenomenology of Spirit, by this very involvement in the natural consciousness, is only an "intelligible form of science" (*P*, §13, *PM*, p. 76). Because it has this form, it conceives itself as the "open road . . . in which science is offered to everyone, and . . . made plain for all" (*ibid.*). The natural consciousness, which at its present stage of development has already arrived, for its own part, at an understanding mode of thought, could therefore "go along with" the experiential history of phenomenal knowledge, and so continue cultivating itself as then in turn to make entry into science as such: "For . . . understanding is thinking, pure activity of the self in general; and what is intelligible is something from the first familiar and common to the scientific and unscientific mind alike, enabling the unscientific mind to enter the domain of science" (*ibid.; PM*, p. 77).[1]

In this entry of the natural consciousness into science, Hegel perceives a peculiar type of cultural event. The task he ascribes to the Phenomenology of Spirit in the Preface, the "task of conducting the individual mind from its unscientific standpoint to that of science" (*P*, §28, *PM*, p. 89),[2] coincides with the definition given in the Introduction, that as a presentation of phenomenal knowledge the Phenomenology is at the same time the "detailed history of the process of training and *educating* consciousness itself up to the level of science" (*I*, §6, *PM*, p. 136).[2a] From this it seems to follow that the Phenomenology itself seeks to provide a presentation of an educational history of the consciousness of spirit on its own account. "Science," so it is said in regard to its first part, the Phenomenology of Spirit (cf. *P*, §35, *PM*, p. 96), "lays before us the morphogenetic process of this cultural development in all its detailed fullness and necessity, and at the same time shows it to be something that has already sunk into the mind as a moment of its being and become a possession of mind. The goal to be reached is the mind's insight into what knowing is" (*P*, §29, *PM*, p. 90). On the other hand, cultural history also appears in the Phenomenology of Spirit as that which already precedes the latter as "actual history," and that in such a way as to be a condition of its existence, i.e., its emergence in time as one phenomenon along with others.[3] Associated with this conception is the fact that "the mind's insight into what knowing is," namely to be absolute knowledge, results in a twofold fashion. Both the presentation of phenomenal knowledge, and also actual history, have absolute knowledge as their goal.[4] Even "actual history," so Hegel declares in the concluding chapter of the *Phenomenology,* is a movement of the spirit "carrying forward this form of knowledge of itself" (*PG*, p. 559; *PM*, p. 801). Actual history is thus the educational history of the universal spirit, in which the latter has brought forth its self-consciousness, and which appears in preserving recollection as a sequence of cultural stages: "While, then, this phase of Spirit begins all over again its formative development, apparently starting solely from itself, yet at the same time it commences at a higher level. The realm of spirits developed in this way, and assuming definite shape in existence, constitutes a succession, where one detaches and sets loose the other, and each takes over from its predecessor the empire of the spiritual world" (*PG*, p. 564; *PM*, p. 808). By contrast, the science of phenomenal knowledge so organizes this same cultural history of absolute spirit, that it can be presented to the natural consciousness of Hegel's time as both necessary and comprehensive, i.e., as complete (cf. §29 of the Preface, already cited, and p. 23 above). It can be stated as a result that the Phenomenology of Spirit does indeed present an educational history, but of such a kind that what appears as its subject is not absolute spirit, but its externalized form, consciousness.

On the question of the meaning of educational history and its relation to phenomenology, a key position is occupied by §28 of the Preface. Every interpretation must start from the fact that here Hegel conjoins the idea of an educational history of the universal spirit, in which the historically later is at the same time the more conceptually elevated, with the notion that at every stage the universal spirit creates a relation to the individual, whose substance this spirit in fact is. Hegel can call the individual uneducated when compared to the standpoint of science, because such a one is governed only by the culture of his time, without having appropriated it scientifically. As the paragraph puts it, we are dealing on the one hand with the twofold relation of the "particular" to the "general" individual, and with that of the mind which "stands higher" to the "lower . . . form of existence" on the other. The general individual therefore appears as subject of the educational process, no less than does the particular. This explains the meaning of the opening sentence of the paragraph: "The task of conducting the individual mind from its unscientific standpoint to that of science had to be taken in its general sense; we had to contemplate the formative development of the universal individual, of self-conscious spirit" (ibid.; PM, p. 89). The context shows that the individual to be educated up to knowledge is intended to be the particular rather than the general one. As such, so we are told a few lines further on, it is "incomplete mind, a concrete shape in whose existence . . . one determinate characteristic predominates, while the others are found only in blurred outline" (ibid.). In the following sentence, Hegel initially breaks off the contrast between particular and general individual, in order to introduce a further distinction: "In that mind which stands higher than another the lower concrete form of existence has sunk into an obscure moment; what was formerly an objective fact is now only a single trace: its definite shape has been veiled, and become simply a piece of shading" (*ibid.*). The relation of general and particular has thereby reverted to a historical relationship, in which the temporally later is at the same time the conceptually higher. The mediating element between them is the concept of moment; the mind which is later than another must stand higher, because it has preserved the earlier in recollection, and is thus richer than the latter. The sentence that follows resumes the first distinction and conjoins it with the second. Before we can enter upon the conjunction, we must first look more closely into the first distinction in Hegel's concept of education.

In the *Philosophical Propaedeutic* of 1809–11, which is closely connected in time with the *Phenomenology of Spirit*, Hegel examined the nature of education in the ascent to universality. The task of the individual is "to elevate his singleness to his universal nature, to educate himself" (*Werke*, XVIII, §41). Anyone who subdues the particularity of his separate and immediately natural existence to his universal, i.e., historically mediated nature, is educated.[5] The necessity of education is founded on the fact that man is more than a merely "natural being" (*ibid.*). Both elements, the ascent to universality and the mediation of immediate naturalness with the universal, are also to be found in the *Phenomenology*'s concept of education, save that here the reference to the upbringing of the natural consciousness to science is the guiding viewpoint and what the *Propaedeutic* calls "universal" is spoken of as "inorganic" nature. This connection is made especially evident in §28 of the Preface. The universal spirit of any particular period is the substance or inorganic nature of the particular individual. The latter educates himself in that he makes the universal which determines him his own, and converts his naturalness into the historical spirit which is reflected in him. "In this respect culture or development of mind, regarded from the side of the individual, consists in his acquiring what lies at his hand ready for him, in making its inorganic nature organic to himself, and taking possession of it for himself. Looked at, however, from the side of universal mind *qua* general spiritual substance, culture means nothing else than that this substance gives itself its own self-consciousness, brings about its own inherent process and its own reflection into self" (*ibid.; PM*, p. 90).[6] We see that, in virtue of the subjectivity of substance, education and the reflection of the universal are associated, in Hegel's view: the cultivation of the universal spirit is reflected in the cultivation of the individual, and thus in the fact that the latter no longer merely lets itself be determined in substance by the stage of cultivation of the universal spirit, but conveys its self-consciousness to this spirit in the scientific ascent toward it.

This is also the point from which to grasp the historical sense of the education of individual consciousness toward the scientific standpoint, as this must be construed from the basic ideas of Preface §28: from the integration of the individual's cultural advance with that of the universal spirit. The education of the individual toward science is the inward recapitulation of the "history of the world's culture." That the true should be essentially a result, is conjoined with the demand to think of substance as subject in such a way that the two educational movements intertwine: that which presently exists, the universal spirit as inorganic nature of the individual, can be acquired only by the roundabout method of again retracing the course of its historical becoming. That is the demand imposed upon the " . . . individual, whose substance is mind at the higher level . . ." (*ibid.; PM*, p. 89). Hegel formulates this notion in the following words: "The particular individual, so far as content is concerned, has also to go through the stages through which the general mind has passed, but as shapes once assumed by mind and now laid aside, as stages of a road which has been worked over and leveled out. Hence it is that, in the case of various kinds of knowledge, we find that what in former days occupied the energies of men of mature mental ability sinks to the level of information, exercise, and even pastimes for children; and in this educational progress we can see the history of the world's

culture delineated in faint outline. This bygone mode of existence has already become an acquired possession of the general
mind, which constitutes the substance of the individual, and,
by thus appearing externally to him, furnishes his inorganic
nature" (ibid.; PM, pp. 89–90). But these well-known observations are not to be understood in an anthropological sense. The
anthropological applications of the idea that the individual has
to recapitulate the cultural history of the universal mind are
already to be found in Kierkegaard, and have become, since
Freud, the common property of depth psychology. That, in
Kierkegaard's words, ". . . the individual is constantly [starting]
all over again . . . , and in him the history of the race" (Werke,
V, Jena 1923, p. 23), already points forward to modern theories
of the interrelation of ontogeny and phylogeny.[7] In contrast to
this, the theme of Hegel's observations is not the recapitulation
of the history of the species in the becoming of the individual,
but rather the conditions the particular individual has to satisfy,
if he wishes to gain possession of the standpoint of science.

In order to perceive this, it is important to realize also the
conditions in whose absence the task set to the Phenomenology,
"of conducting the individual mind from its unscientific
standpoint to that of science" (PM, p. 89), would be insoluble.
For the philosopher there emerges from this task the demand
so to organize the sequence of cultural shapes, that the individual advancing toward science is also able to follow their presentation. But that this task can be accomplished, is also rooted,
as Hegel sees it, in the fact that the history of the education of
universal mind has reached a stage at which the principle of
science is also the principle of natural consciousness, or of the
particular individual. If this be presupposed, it can be said that
science is the telos of the natural consciousness (cf. above, pp.
27 f.). This particular relationship of consciousness and science
now needs to be specified in greater detail.

We have emphasized before this, that because it seeks to be a
preparatory and introductory science, which in this sense only
"comes on the scene," the Phenomenology of Spirit has itself
reduced itself to the level of "appearance." It emerged, further-

more, that understanding, for Hegel, is the mediating factor between natural consciousness and science. This means that the reduction to appearance now takes on the nature of a lowering to the educational level of the understanding. The natural consciousness is to evolve toward "reason" by way of the understanding, in the particular sense which Hegel attaches to these terms. The importance of the task here confronting the Phenomenology of Spirit, and the very definite "strategy" leading to its fulfillment, can be brought out more clearly still if we seek to explain the situation that would obtain if the Phenomenology did not exist. In that case the natural consciousness of the cultural stage contemporary with Hegel, and science as such, would stand confronted without understanding one another: "Each of these two sides takes the other to be the perversion of the truth" (*P,* §26; *PM,* p. 87). Let us examine this situation more closely.

In the *"immediate certainty* of self" the natural consciousness —as we have already noted—possesses itself as "absolute form" (*ibid.; PM,* p. 87). This form provides for it the basis of the "absolute independence, which [it] knows [it] possesses in every type and phase of knowledge"; as "unconditioned being" it possesses in its self-certainty "the principle of its reality." From the standpoint of this reality, the shape of the scientific system must have for it the "character of unreality," the "element" in which science moves must appear to it "a remote and distant region, in which consciousness is no longer in possession of itself" (*ibid.*).

Conversely, science as such must rank as *"opposite"* to the standpoint of natural consciousness, "that of knowing about objective things as opposed to itself, and about itself as opposed to them." That this principle should rank, to the natural consciousness, as the principle of reality, must appear to a completed science "as the loss of mind altogether," and yet science as such "presupposes or demands" from self-consciousness that it betake itself into the element proper to science, that it shall "have risen into [the] high ether" appropriate thereto "in order to be able to live with science, and in science, and really to feel alive there" (*ibid.*).

This, then, is the constellation obtaining between natural consciousness and science. But if it is all a matter of rescuing the individual at the stage of culture contemporary with Hegel from the prevailing state of duality, a "ladder" must also be extended to him, so that he can climb upward to science. Hegel acknowledges, for this very reason, that "the individual has the right to demand" that science shall "hold the ladder to help him to get at least as far as this position" (*ibid.*). Hegel recognizes, indeed—and herein lies the particular "strategy" whereby he carries out the task assigned to the Phenomenology of Spirit, namely to provide this "ladder"—that the "standpoint" of science is in fact already that of the natural consciousness, so that it is simply a question of showing the individual that "he has in himself this ground to stand on" (*ibid.*). But how can the standpoint of science be exhibited in natural consciousness? By showing, through a presentation of phenomenal knowledge, that the very "element" which constitutes the ground of science is no other than that which constitutes the reality-principle of natural consciousness, namely "absolute form," the principle of self-consciousness. We remarked earlier (cf. p. 28 above) that the "vindication" undertaken by the Phenomenology of Spirit consists in demonstrating that natural consciousness is in essence already destined toward absolute knowledge, the concept of knowledge as its *telos*. We can now see that the fact that self-consciousness realizes itself as "thinking"—albeit in the form of understanding—bears witness to an "element" which necessarily lends itself to development into absolute knowledge, and thus into the scientific system which absolute knowledge presents. Here, indeed, lies the reason why natural consciousness should be able in its own element to develop into absolute knowledge; what it will require to accomplish will—as we saw—be the surrender of its "naturalness"; it will then be able to develop from understanding to reason, or from unscientific consciousness to scientific cognition.

The *Phenomenology of Spirit* fulfills its task by unfolding this "element" of certainty or knowing self-relation. This element "only attains its perfect meaning and acquires transparency through the process of gradually developing it" (*P*, §26; *PM*, p. 86).[8] As we have seen, presentation is as such the process of this becoming. At the end of the road it has evolved into "knowing in the universal sense" and thus into absolute knowledge. But this occurs in the *Phenomenology of Spirit* only through its having fully unfolded in the object of presentation, phenomenal knowledge. Since—as we were just saying—it is "self-consciousness" which constitutes this element, it is a matter of self-consciousness also attaining through this process its "perfect meaning and transparency." It receives this through the history of experience which it undergoes, as phenomenal knowledge, in an increasingly perspicuous manner, until it reaches its goal. Now it is of the greatest importance to notice that Hegel has defined this "element" common both to the understanding natural consciousness and to science as "reflection." "Reflection" was a term used in many senses both in physics and also in psychology and logic; in post-Kantian philosophy it played an important role. Without at present entering into the conceptual history of this term, it is nonetheless necessary, in view of its diversity of meanings, to bring out the sense in which Hegel speaks of reflection in the *Phenomenology of Spirit*. It thereupon appears that in the *Phenomenology* he no longer uses this term in the sense that he employed in the *Differenzschrift*. Hegel there describes the contemporary philosophy he is attacking as "reflection-philosophy," but in another sense of the term he also calls "true" speculation a reflection. In the *Phenomenology of Spirit*, however, the name "reflection" designates a structure of self-consciousness conceived in Cartesian terms. We have already characterized the structure of self-consciousness as that of a movement in which the *subjectum* "represents" to itself a "given" *objectum* in such a way that it refers equally to this object—as its other—and to itself as the "self" which has become self-certain in and through this reference. We have seen, moreover, that the "naturalness" of self-consciousness lies in this "givenness" of the *objectum* which determines the self. We noted that it is of the essence of natural consciousness, as self-consciousness, that it is able to absolve itself from this bond. Once absolution is achieved, the self has attained to a power set free from all determinations, and is no longer "consciousness" in the usual sense, but has become an absolute subject. This development can also be described in the terminology of "reflection." Reflection of the self upon itself, the *cogito me cogitare* of Descartes, is a movement whereby the essence of selfhood emerges as the *res cogitans,* which already in Descartes—through the experiment of doubt—has been largely able to demonstrate its independence of the givenness of "reality." The enormous power that this I has, to direct itself with the help of representation upon everything possible, and thereby to transcend the immediacy of the merely sensory relation to the given, as a "reality" given to the senses, and to persist in a self-enclosed self-reference, was then raised to a "principle" during the subsequent phase of thought. Kant, who on the one hand gave warning against reflection as a thinking unrelated to objects, since it could lead to a habit of groundless and sophistical speculation, was responsible, on the other hand, through his transcendental philosophy, for opening the road to the idealist position, insofar as he had freed subjectivity, as the logical principle of a "pure" I, from the given. In the early writings of Fichte and Schelling this pure transcendental I is already elevated into the "absolute" I, which is able, by the power of its reflection as a making-possible of itself (as a *causa sui*), to "generate" after its fashion not only itself, but, by means of its positings, the whole (cf. the development of the history of German Idealism briefly outlined above). It is therefore inherent in the structure of reflection, and thus in the subjecthood of any natural consciousness, to be able to evolve into the "absolute subject," and it is on this, more specifically, that the "strategy" of the Phenomenology of Spirit depends. That self-consciousness realizes itself as reflection, signifies as follows: The "other," this seemingly "existing" given, to which I relate in the cognitive representation of my self-consciousness, proves to be something that I can eliminate or negate by the act of this representing—

for example, by my doubting it. It thus has its "reality" as an "other" only in and through this cognitive reference back to myself (reflection), which in turn reverts upon itself in the very same act (reflection), and thereby becomes certain of itself and of what it knows. This reflecting is the "element" that ordinary common sense moves in, and all philosophical cognition at the level of understanding as well. The same "element," however, also underlies the concept of knowledge, the Idea of philosophy as such, save only that it has still to attain clarity, and become an "ether" unclouded by anything alien. This does not in fact take place by way of any abstraction from the alien material, but occurs, rather, when consciousness sees through the difference between its reflection and a non-reflective otherness independent of this, as an illusion: otherness or objectivity is in truth itself reflection, a relating-to-an-other which at the same time relates to itself. It is therefore not the opposite of its reflection which consciousness relates to when it reflects. For as reflection it again finds itself in the other. Reflection is thus a movement which overlaps both the subject-side and the object-side. Only when reflection has proved itself to be such a movement, in which both subject and object, as moments thereof, are themselves posited and superseded, has it become the element of absolute knowledge. This process itself is to be brought about by the movement constituting the Phenomenology of Spirit. It confers complete translucency on the element, namely reflection. Once completion is attained, reflection is the element of science itself. Hegel describes this element as "a self having knowledge purely of itself in the absolute antithesis of itself" (*P*, §26; *PM*, p. 86).[9] This is to say that it is that reflection which finds itself, *qua* cognitive relation, in the other, but in such a way that, in and with this relation, the other is at the same time brought into the self, so that this self thereby proves itself a principle which possesses itself in total freedom from any determinacy on the part of "nature," and exists in complete self-mastery in the "absoluteness" so understood. It "exists" as that element which is able to uplift to itself, in its own "ether," all "immediacy"—meaning, for Hegel, the category of "being"—

because in virtue of the representing relation this immediacy constitutes in truth an otherness to it, which, as the other of the representing subject, is grounded in a reflection of that subject. It is part of the Idea of the Phenomenology of Spirit to demonstrate that the knowing of the natural consciousness takes place as a reflection, and that if it would only adhere consistently to this character of its knowledge, it would be bound almost automatically to push on to that existence in which, liberated from all naturalness or anything "alien," it would take on a shape in which "appearance becomes identified with essence" (sc. with reflection properly understood) (*I*, §17; *PM*, p. 145).[10] The account of cognition seeks to "demonstrate" to the consciousness of Hegel's own day that every natural consciousness is capable of this. It seeks to show this contemporary consciousness that it, too, could get there, if it were consistently to take the path pursued by phenomenal knowledge as the object of this presentation.

Before seeking to delineate in more detail the "method" of this route of phenomenal knowledge, as a "pathway of experience," and the mode of presenting that pathway, let us first explain, on the basis of our insight into the nature of self-consciousness as reflection, what exactly the supposedly false view of reflection was in the philosophies of Hegel's time, which made necessary the effort of giving this presentation here.

NOTES

1. "For the understanding is thinking, the pure ego; and the sensible is the already familiar and that which science and the unscientific have in common—that whereby the latter can immediately enter science" (*K*, p. 382).

2. "The task of leading the individual from his uneducated standpoint to knowledge . . ." (*K*, p. 402).

2a. ". . . is the detailed history of consciousness' own education to the level of science" (*D*, p. 54).

3. On the problem of an immanent justification of science by way of an independent history of culture, cf. Fulda, *Das Problem einer Ein-*

leitung in Hegels Wissenschaft der Logik, Frankfurt 1965, pp. 217 ff., 251 ff. Fulda sets out from the encyclopaedic structure of the Hegelian philosophy, which provides him with the clue to the question of what task can be assigned, from within the system, to the *Phenomenology* of 1807. There is no need to discuss here in detail Fulda's distinction between four senses of history and historicity in Hegel's philosophy (history of absolute spirit, world history, history of philosophy, and history of culture), since the differentiated concept of history in the system of the *Encyclopaedia* is not yet to be found in the *Phenomenology* of 1807. World history and the cultural history of the universal spirit merge, in the *Phenomenology of Spirit,* into a unity, which as "real" history is contrasted to, and at the same time limited by, the history of the education of consciousness into science which is presented in the *Phenomenology* itself.

4. Jürgen Habermas, in *Erkenntnis und Interesse* (Frankfurt 1968), has seen the goal of the entire movement of the *Phenomenology* in the recapitulation of the cultural history of the race as a history of emancipation. He has failed to notice that the goal of the *Phenomenology* can be concerned with nothing else but the unfolding of self-consciousness in its *truth.* This truth, according to the Preface, is nothing else but the whole of the scientific system. Self-consciousness knowing itself in its truth, i.e., as the system of its own determinations, is absolute knowledge. It will not do to exclude the absolute and absolute knowledge from the *Phenomenology of Spirit,* and yet to employ the latter as a "model" for a movement of emancipation.

5. Cf. on this point H. G. Gadamer, *Wahrheit und Methode,* Tübingen (2nd ed.) 1965, pp. 8 ff. Gadamer emphasizes that the sublation of naturalness essential to Hegel's concept of culture signifies a historical mediation with the substance of ethical spirit, which is completed only in the absolute sublation of substantial otherness performed by philosophy: "For cultivation, as the movement of alienation and appropriation, terminates, for Hegel, in a complete mastery of substance, in that dissolution of all objecthood which is first attained in the absolute knowledge of philosophy" (*ibid.,* p. 12).

6. "In this respect, education, considered from the point of view of the individual, consists in his acquiring what is thus given to him; he must digest his inorganic nature and take possession of it for himself. But from the point of view of the general spirit as the substance this means nothing else than that this should acquire self-consciousness and produce its becoming and reflection in itself" (*K,* p. 402).

7. For Kierkegaard, the anthropological application of the Hegelian dialectic of individual and substantial spirit offers the possibility of coupling in thought the Christian dogma of original sin with the freedom of man to do evil.

8. ". . . receives its perfection and transparence only through the movement of its becoming" (*K*, p. 398).

9. ". . . pure self-recognition in absolute otherness . . ." (*K*. p. 398).

10. ". . . its appearance becomes equal to its essence . . ." (*D*, p. 26).

IV

Reflection-Philosophy and Absolute Reflection

THE STAGE of culture contemporary with Hegel can be described as a "reflection culture." At the outset of the new epoch, the "beginning of the new spirit," it had already been generally recognized that the essence of self-consciousness lies in "reflection"; insofar as reflection took place as philosophy, it was recognized as a "rational" form of reflection. But according to Hegel, this philosophizing reflection was still an exercise of the understanding. For in it—as he tried to show in his journal articles—it was only the power of self-consciousness to divide and oppose which was essentially brought into play. It went unnoticed that the oppositions arising on the basis of such division derived from an identity of the subjectivity and objectivity of the self, and that for this very reason the tendency must prevail for such oppositions to revert to identity. Only the movement of such a reversion to identity, uniting the opposites, would constitute an exercise of reason. Even where people were already attempting this, in accordance with the "new spirit," and were beginning to take note of the unifying power of the self, the absoluteness of this power had not yet—so Hegel thought—been discerned; the severance of subject and object arising from the opposition had therefore not really been posited "in the absolute—as its appearance . . . as life." But in this the young Hegel already saw, in the *Differenzschrift*, the "task of philosophy" (*Werke*, I, p. 177). In contrast to the reflection merely exercised as understanding, which for him was simply the power of "limiting" or determining, he therefore attempted to arrive at a reflection which could serve as an "instrument of philosophizing" (*op. cit.*, p. 178), and might answer to the "need of philosophy" (*ibid.*, pp. 172 ff., 177). The road to this, which might enable self-consciousness—as reflective understanding—to ascend beyond itself to a rational form of reflection, he still saw there in the possibility of "seducing" (cf. *ibid.*, p. 178) the understanding into an infinite completion of its limited determinations (cf. *ibid.*, p. 179). We have no need to demonstrate in more detail here, how in so doing the understanding "destroys" itself, and by this very fact raises itself from itself to reason (cf. *ibid.*)—and this in such a way that the oppositions are not in fact abolished, but construed into identity as an appearance of the absolute (*ibid.*, p. 201). The method of a reflection realizing itself as reason was still seen there by Hegel —following Schelling [1]—in conjunction with a "transcendental intuition" (cf. *ibid.*, pp. 194 ff.) which is able to effect a "synthesis of opposites" (*ibid.*, p. 195) and to that extent constitutes the "positive side" of speculative knowledge or reason.

Now what is the method of the *Phenomenology of Spirit,* published six years later? We no longer hear anything there about transcendental intuition, though we do about reflection. And here, indeed—as we have seen already—reflection is defined as the "element" which science as such, the scientific system, possesses as its pure "ether"; reflection consummates itself as the absolute subject, insofar as its "knowledge in universal form" is *"knowledge purely of itself* in absolute otherness to itself" (*P*, §26, *PM*, p. 86, [amended]. Author's italics. See n. 9, Ch. III above). We have seen already that this very element, reflection, only acquires "its perfection and . . . transparence" (*ibid.* [amended]. See n. 8, Ch. III) through the movement of its becoming, and hence that reflection, though not yet in perfect form, also constitutes the element of the Phenomenology of Spirit. Now we stressed at the outset of this discussion that there is a difference, a "separation," between the Phenomenology of Spirit as the science which is realized as presentation, and its object, the phenomenal knowledge to be found in experience. We must therefore ask separately, on the one hand, in what way does reflection, as the element of phenomenology, determine the presentation? and on the other hand, how does it determine its object, phenomenal knowledge? In a more general sense, however, it is also possible to obtain from the Preface an answer which seems to have validity for presenting science and phenomenal knowledge alike, and leads us into a discussion of the phenomenology's method, which has to be conceived in terms of its element, namely reflection.[2]

In §17 of the Preface, Hegel has set forth the program which governs the whole of his philosophizing: "In my view—a view which the developed exposition of the system itself can alone justify—everything depends on grasping and expressing the true not as *substance* but as *subject* as well." In the course of our discussion of "cultural history" we have already frequently referred to the Cartesian conception of consciousness. From the perspective of the development of "spirit" traced out in the Preface (see below, p. 53),.this stage is typified by the fact that spirit has divided itself up into "two aspects—cognition and objectivity which is . . . negative of . . . knowing" (*P*, §36; *PM*, p. 96), and this by the power of the negative, which first appeared as this "dissimilarity . . . between ego and object" (*P*, §37, *PM*, p. 97). In this form the object is an "other" to the knowing subject, but already at this stage philosophy has recognized that this other is an other "in thought" (cf. *P*, §29; *PM*, p. 91), that the content of presentations is ultimately taken up into thought-determinations, which in their totality constitute "substance." For Spinoza, substance was the absolute, or *causa sui*. By contrast, at the onset of the "new spirit," made explicit for Hegel in idealist philosophizing since Kant, philosophy began to see the absolute, no longer in substance, but in the power of self-consciousness, in the subject, to which, however, substance still remained contrasted as "object." This fixed opposition between the two sides of subject and object had therefore to be overcome, and this in virtue of the insight that subject, as the absolute, must have power over substance. But the element of this powerful self is reflection; so it was necessary to show that reflection is also at work on the side of substance, and thus of the object, or objectivity. In his *System of Transcendental Idealism* of 1800 Schelling had attempted to show this by presenting a genetic account, in which substance—in his case regarded as nature —raises itself in ascending power from matter to self-consciousness, and thus to reflection. But this genesis of nature (substance) represented a sequence distinct from and opposite to the genesis of self-consciousness (to nature). Whereas in the *Differenzschrift* Hegel had still declared for this dualistic system, he tried, in the *Phenomenology of Spirit,* to show in a single history of experience that and how substance *itself* reflects itself, and thus already exhibits therein the subject to which the element of reflection pertains. For Spinoza, "thought" was only *one* of the attributes of substance, the other being extension. Since, for Hegel, extension is subject to the power of thought, in that it can in fact be "sublated" by the latter, he considers substance itself—and not merely as attribute—to be thought. Thought, however, is the mode of exercise of the absolute *qua* self; and thus the movement from the side of substance must be so viewed "that this substance gives itself its own self-consciousness, brings about its own inherent process and its own reflection into self" (*P,* §28; *PM,* p. 90).

Now if reflection is already the element of phenomenal knowledge, it must be part of its experiential history that on the side of the object standing opposite to the knower, there is also "experience" of the movement in which this totality of thought-determinations, substance, reflects itself. It must be experienced as the movement in which substance, not yet known as concept, but at first presented as an unmoved self-identity which immediately determines consciousness, sets itself into a non-identity, whence reflection, however, leads back to a new identity. This "reflection in itself," this movement which we shall later explain in more detail, is initially experienced as an activity pertaining to the object-side alone; but then the consciousness engaged in experience slowly begins—in the course of its further "education"—to perceive increasingly that in truth reflection is not operating on two opposing sides, but that the whole is a process of the self. But this it knows expressly only at the end of the road, once it has acquired the existence of absolute knowledge. Only then, when all "substantial content" has likewise come to be "directly in the possession of the ego," and that means when being, or substance, for its part, has taken on "the character of self, or the concept," "the Phenomenology of Spirit concludes" (P, §37; PM, p. 97 [adapted]). The program of the Phenomenology must therefore be so understood, that phenomenal knowledge, as it appears in the opposition of subject and the "other," namely substance, brings this very opposition to identity by way of "experience." It thence appears that, even on the side of substance, the subject, reflection, was always already at work, which is just why "everything depends on grasping and expressing the ultimate truth not as substance, but as subject as well" (P, §17; PM, p. 80).[3] The particular determinations under which the subject requires "grasping and expressing" have already been stated by Hegel in the Preface. To obtain a better insight into the nature of the subject as absolute reflection, we shall elucidate some of these determinations in what follows.

The basic determinations constituting the nature of the subject, and its subjectivity, are all determinations of the movement in which, for Hegel, the "dialectic" of the self-moving "concept" lies. To the extent, then, that subject and the unfolding of the dialectical concept are one and the same, we shall discover more about Hegel's concept of the concept. The basic determinations of the dialectical movement are sublation, mediation, and negativity.

1. The subject unfolds itself as a positing. Its first posit (thesis) is that of the immediacy (unmediatedness) in which knowing (representing) and its object are "one" in identity; and thus the positing in a "self-identical" (cf. P, §55; PM, p. 114) determination, which may be called either "immediately universal" (cf. P, §20; PM, p. 82) or "subsistent substance" (cf. P, §54; PM, p. 113).

2. In a next step, resulting from the reflection of the subject, it

splits itself (by analyzing, cf. *P*, §32; *PM*, p. 92) as positing knowledge from its determination. It posits itself as a self "over against" the latter. This separating counter-positing is—as we have already seen—reflection in the manner of the "understanding"; the understanding carries out the work of the "negative," insofar as this counter-positing is a supersession of immediacy, its annihilation in the sense of "*tollere.*" But this negative appears not merely "as a dissimilarity . . . between ego and object," for it is "just as much the inequality of the substance with itself" (*P*, §37; *PM*, p. 97). The power of the negative also converts the determinacy of substance, which as selfsameness had a continuing existence, into dissimilarity, and thus into "dissolution" (*P*, §54; *PM*, p. 113). This dissolution now seems to take place automatically only to the one side, namely that opposed to the self, because the knowing or thinking of the self is now distinguished from this side. But the fact is, that this power of the negative is ultimately nothing else but an activity of the self, since as self it is the negative (cf. *P*, §54, 21; *PM*, pp. 113, 82), so that it may also be said that it is the thinking operating on this side, which effects this dissolution of selfsameness into dissimilarity (cf. *P*, §§54 and 55; *PM*, pp. 113, 115). The dissolution is the work of thought (*nous, P*, §55; *PM*, p. 114), and consists in the fact that every selfsameness (identity) is such only because it continues to maintain itself in a delimiting relation to dissimilarity, "having its own otherness within itself," so that as a positing, this step of reflection is nothing else but the positing of this otherness. Reflection thus proves to be likewise a movement on the side of the object, resulting in an opposition between the determinations of selfsameness and otherness, as well as being one which brings self and object into contrast. We thus find ourselves at the stage of antithesis.

However, this antithetical process already furnishes the beginning of a "mediation." To be sure, it is only a true mediation if

3. the third step of reflection is taken, if the self (the subject) "finds itself again" in its objecthood, otherness or objectivity, and in this sense returns to itself, realizes itself as "reflection into the otherness of its own self" (*P*, §18; *PM*, pp. 80–81), as "having

pure knowledge of itself in absolute otherness" (*P,* §26; *PM,* p. 86 [amended]), and is absolute reflection.

This "reflection into self" (*P,* §21; *PM,* p. 82) is nothing else but "the self" which, reverting into itself, is now really "for itself" (*ibid.*), and purely executes the movement of "mediating with its own self its transitions from one . . . position to the opposite" (*P,* §18; *PM,* p. 80). "Negativity" once again brings about this pure act of return—but now by the fact that the preceding negation, which brought about the dissolution and preservation of dissimilarity, is again negated. Negativity, determined as the double negation, is self-identity "reinstating" itself. Insofar as the antithetical position constitutes the untrue, what appears as a result through the becoming of the whole is the "true" (*ibid.*). Becoming, in the process, has "sublated" itself from thesis, by way of antithesis, to synthesis—as a sort of conservation and transformation, an elevation (*conservare et elevare*). The self-identity thereby "working itself out through an active self-directed process" (*P,* §21; *PM,* p. 82), or "reflection into its own self," designates the nature of a self-completing "mediation" which has mediated the non-identity of that antithesis into a new identity, an identity which includes the old identity and this non-identity within itself, to form an identity of identity and non-identity.

The self which realizes itself in the shape of reflection is called the "subject." The subjectivity of the subject is determined by this movement of sublation, negativity, and mediation; these are therefore the basic determinations under which the dialectical movement of thesis, antithesis, and synthesis takes place; and hence the subject is synonymous with the concept. We were told that the motto of the Phenomenology consisted, in Hegel's view, in expressing the true not as substance only, but as subject as well. From the standpoint of substance, this implies that in it the "labour of the negative" (*P,* §19; *PM,* p. 81) must be carried out; it must be transformed into a "living" substance (*P,* §18; *PM,* p. 80). The further significance of this in the history of philosophy—namely that the Cartesian *res extensa,* which was separated from thinking by an abyss, and the Spinozistic substance, in which thinking inhered merely as an attribute, must be shown to be posited and moved by thinking—does not need to be further pursued at present. But let us recall once more that, for Hegel, the self is nothing else but the transcendental apperception of Kant, which is able to form and order according to a priori rules, namely the categories. Although Kant may still have derived these categories from the Aristotelian table of judgments, in German Idealism, and for Hegel especially, they had to be derived from the self which had emerged as reason; or more correctly, the self as "subject" derived them from itself in its own self-movement, and presented them as the scientific system in the completeness of its interconnection. This presentation is the "true shape" in which truth exists (cf. *P*, §§5, 18, 19, 25, 38, 53; *PM*, pp. 70, 80–82, 85–86, 97–98, 111), namely absolute truth in the form of "science" proper.

NOTES

1. On Hegel's relation to Schelling in the *Differenzschrift*, cf. the author's *Die Bestimmung der Philosophie im Deutschen Idealismus*, Stuttgart 1964; and more recently, his *Vernunft und Welt* (Phaenomenologica No. 36), The Hague 1970, pp. 1 ff; (English version in *Reason and World*, The Hague 1971).

2. On the meaning of reflection in the *Phenomenology of Spirit*, cf. R. Bubner's recent "Philosophie ist ihre Zeit, in Gedanken gefasst," in *Hermeneutik und Dialektik, Hans-Georg Gadamer zum 70. Geburtstag*, Tübingen 1970, vol. I, pp. 317–43 (esp. pp. 333 ff.).

3. ". . . everything depends on this, that we comprehend and express the true not as substance but just as much as subject" (*K*, p. 388).

V

Consciousness and Spirit

As a "PREPARATION" for science proper, the *Phenomenology of Spirit* has—as we have seen—a twofold task: in the first place, it is to bring forth the "concept of science" in the shape of absolute knowledge (and this as a realization of absolute reflection); in the second, it is to persuade the natural consciousness of Hegel's own day, which seeks to progress toward science, that its element is none other than the principle of natural consciousness. This second task is to be fulfilled by demonstrating or "presenting" to the natural consciousness how it is able to evolve into absolute knowledge in the shapes of consciousness peculiar to "phenomenal knowledge," by testing its current claim to grasp the truth and repeatedly perceiving this to be in error, until it has reached that form of knowledge which is no longer exposed to error, but is absolute. Since "consciousness . . . comprehends nothing but what falls within its experience" (*P*, §36; *PM*, p. 96 and *PG*, p. 558; *PM*, p. 800), this presentation must be that of a history of experiences.

This second task of the Phenomenology is connected with the first, inasmuch as the presentation of the history of experience is nothing else but the history of the generation of the "concept of knowledge." It seems—at first anyway—to be possible for the Phenomenology to be able to "delegate" both tasks wholly to phenomenal knowledge, so that—as is even expressly said at one point—"all we are left to do is simply and solely to look on" (*I*, §13; *PM*, p. 141).[1] More detail on this point must be gathered from the "method of carrying . . . out" the inquiry (*I*, §9; *PM*, p. 139), as it is explained in the Introduction.

As we have noted already, phenomenal knowledge, in contrast to "natural consciousness *per se*," is qualified by the fact that it is "taken along" by the presentation on the road leading to the specific "goal" "fixed" for it (*I*, §8; *PM*, p. 137). But this "being taken along" does not yet imply that phenomenal knowledge would behave entirely passively; on the contrary, it is shown how it actively takes a stand "against" untruth (*I*, §6; *PM*, p. 136). It seeks ever more strongly to liberate itself from the bonds constituted by its "inorganic" nature (see above, p. 3). In its shape at any given time, it does not merely subject its truth-claim to a "methodic doubt," such as was first undertaken in modern philosophy in the *Meditations* of Descartes, a doubt which soon falls back into assurance of the self's own certainty, as that known by it. If a real independence of all determinations and the absolute power of a self-determination are to be attained, the doubt must become a "despair" (*ibid.*), and dissolve all "natural views, thoughts, and opinions," in short, all modes of givenness, which hold consciousness in that "division" which determines the contemporary natural consciousness. The method designed for the realization of such a "despair" is "skepticism," albeit not that which, like classical skepticism, remains rooted in the mere setting-up of oppositions and contradictions. It is, rather, a skepticism which in radical fashion doubts everything known to it, which is "directed to the whole compass of phenomenal consciousness" (*ibid.*), in order to uncover the contradictions prevailing in each of its shapes, and by doing so to demolish naturalness and attain to perfect "presuppositionlessness." This skepticism is so radical that it is finally also able to question itself as well, its own skeptical attitude as a "standard," and only thereby does it prove itself capable of attaining to a perfect, presuppositionless, absolute knowledge; in just this sense it is a "self-realizing skepticism." This radical attitude qualifies phenomenal knowledge, in contrast to "natural consciousness *per se*." For this alone has made its spirit "skilled" in really examining what truth is, and in

51

determining itself along the road by this self-examination; the natural consciousness, *per se,* which does not take a radical attitude, remains incapable of this and so cannot take the road which leads to absolute knowledge. But how is phenomenal knowledge capable of this "despair," and of the method of self-realizing skepticism? The reason for it is to be sought in the principle of phenomenal consciousness. But what does this principle consist in, which makes this consciousness capable of such a radical testing of itself and such a further determination with the aim of absolute knowledge? Hegel's answer is, that it lies in its nature as concept. Self-consciousness made conscious is the concept, and as such is able to grasp its nature. Hence Hegel's lapidary phrase in this connection: "Consciousness, however, is to itself its own notion" (*I*, §8; *PM,* p. 138).[2]

We cannot even approximately explain in this context Hegel's difficult doctrine of the concept. It must suffice to recall once more (see above, pp. xx, 8) that Kant had already recognized the structure of self-consciousness as that of an "original synthetic unity of apperception," the unity of the "I think." In his later works, especially in the *Science of Logic,* Hegel will expressly refer to this Kantian account of self-consciousness and define the logical structure of self-consciousness as that of the concept (cf. *WL,* II, 221; *HSL,* p. 584). Now at the start of the "road" of the presentation of the *Phenomenology of Spirit,* the concept has certainly not yet attained to an existence which—as Hegel was later to write (cf. *WL,* II, 220; *HSL,* p. 583)—moves in the freedom of its "unrestricted equality with itself"; and yet—precisely because it is "for itself" the concept—consciousness is already able, for all its limitations, to criticize its standards and presuppositions by means of a conceiving not yet transparent to itself, and by this very critique to evolve into the shape of absolute knowledge.

To discern this more fully, we must discuss the method whereby this critique takes place in the Phenomenology. To do this we must first explain—as Hegel does—what "knowledge" really is, particularly in relation to its object, and what is meant by that "truth" in the light of which consciousness critically examines itself.

The Introduction lists the "abstract" determinations, and does so in the form in which they are "taken up into consciousness," [3] and "as they are immediately offered to us" (cf. *I*, §10; *PM*, p. 140). The Preface, on the other hand—which must be read in conjunction with the closing sections of the *Phenomenology*— sets forth the determinations exhibited by the movement of spirit, as it mediates and becomes concrete to itself; here we shall make reference to both. But that raises the question—which we shall have to deal with in advance—as to how these two aspects of the Phenomenology, as science of the experience of consciousness and as science of the phenomenal spirit, are related to one another.

The question whether the Phenomenology of Spirit really does split up into two parts, a science of experience and a science of spirit, has long been a preoccupation of Hegelian research. Of late the controversy has been renewed with many arguments previously left unnoticed. We take the view that the Phenomenology of Spirit is from beginning to end both a science of experience and a science of spirit. And from this we deem ourselves entitled to draw upon the Preface for an interpretation of the "method" of the Phenomenology, although it may possibly be valid only for a stretch of the pathway of presentation.

This is in no way to dispute, however, that the architectonic of the *Phenomenology* contains gaps which Hegelian research has not yet been able to account for; to speak of a strictly unitary conception of the Phenomenology would certainly not be correct. Yet we think it possible to show that in the Introduction as in the text, in the chapter on spirit as in the Preface added after the work's completion, Hegel conceived the Phenomenology throughout as a science of experience and a science of spirit. Because it relates to the experience of consciousness, the science of spirit is a science of experience.

Before seeking to pursue this demonstration under specific headings (see below, p. 62), we must be rid of the indefiniteness which has so far still characterized the use of the term "spirit." What, then, properly belongs to the concept of that which Hegel has designated as "spirit"? In order to clear this up, we must reach out beyond the text of the Preface and draw upon the final chapter of the *Phenomenology*.

1. The Concept of Spirit

What is of most importance about the concept of spirit * in the *Phenomenology* is that it is comprehended as the unity of substance and subject—whereby the unity increasingly realizes itself in historical shapes. "Substance" here means initially "ethical substance" (*PG,* p. 314; *PM,* p. 458) or the "ethical life of a peo-ple" (*PG,* p. 315; *PM,* p. 460). This ethical substance of a people, which permeates and determines the doings of all individuals, is as such already in unity with the "self," which is essentially activity. But this unity of substance and subject, the mores and customs existing and prevailing on their own, like their realiza-tion in the "action of all" (*PG,* p. 314; *PM,* p. 458), is still imme-diate and to some extent unconscious: the spirit still "has to advance to the consciousness of what it is immediately" (*PG,* p. 315; *PM,* p. 460). Since ethical substance is what Hegel describes, from the Heidelberg *Encyclopaedia* on, as "objective spirit," [4] while the "actual self-consciousness" of spirit (*PG,* p. 316; *PM,* p. 461) is already referred to in the *Phenomenology* as "absolute spirit," it is possible, with Jean Hyppolite,[5] to look back from the later version of the system and to say that "spirit" in the *Phenomenology* is nothing else but the experience of ob-jective spirit, whereby it becomes absolute spirit. The various stages whereby spirit attains to consciousness of itself cannot be pursued here in detail. In the three main phases of the chapter entitled "Spirit," the sections on ethical order, culture, and mo-rality, there is first of all a separation of the "individual self"

* *Geist,* in J. B. Baillie's much used translation of the *Phenomenol-ogy,* is translated most often as "mind"; others translate *Geist* as "spirit." In this book both "mind" and "spirit" are used interchange-ably for *Geist.*—ED.

from objective spirit, which rises to an "alienation" : the self perceives the customs and institutions of the community no longer as the action and work of all, but as an alien reality. But in the progress of experience, the completed "process of estrangement" (*PG*, p. 423; *PM*, p. 613) is transformed into a new identity: in that self-consciousness recognizes the "general will" as the true essence of a people's institutions—a process which takes place, historically, during the period of the French Revolution—its "certainty of self" becomes for it "the essence of all . . . spiritual spheres . . . and all reality is solely spirituality" (*PG*, p. 415; *PM*, p. 600). But in this identity the spirit's self-cognition is still by no means completed. For in that the self seeks to make this knowledge of the spirituality of the real into a standard for its behavior—which for Hegel constitutes the essence of the "moral world-view"—it arrives once more at a "contradiction between its pure self and the necessity felt by this self to externalize itself and turn into something actual" (*PG*, p. 470; *PM*, p. 676). For the actualization always signifies a clash with the pure universality and selfsameness of the spiritual—here understood as "duty." This is a contradiction in which, according to Hegel, both the Kantian and Fichtean moral philosophy of his day, and also the pietistic ideal of the "beautiful soul," are bound to become involved. The "reconciliation" of this contradiction between the pure universality of its self-knowledge and the singleness of all action and realization is achieved only at the level of "religion," at which the "self-contained and self-sufficient reality" (*PG*, p. 314; *PM*, p. 458) [6] underlying everything actual is apprehended not only as pure knowledge, but as "absolutely self-confined *single individual*" (*PG*, p. 471; *PM*, p. 677). It is well known that in the section on religion Hegel conjoined what in the later system of the *Encyclopaedia* constitutes two separate forms of absolute spirit: art and religion. The reason for this is that, for Hegel, Greek art—insofar as it subdues the divine to the presentative activity of the subject—represents a decisive step in the direction of a "subjectivization" of the divine, which in Oriental nature-religion is still understood wholly in terms of substance. This process, however, is completed only in the "revealed religion" of Christianity, to which,—as Hegel brings out in the Preface—the concept of "spirit" properly "belongs." It is above all the representation of an incarnation, in which "God is beheld sensuously and immediately as a self, as a real individual human being" (*PG*, p. 528; *PM*, p. 758). In this representation, "the divine being is known as spirit," not only because here it is immediately viewed as "self-confined single individual" but also because the incarnation of God signifies—admittedly still in pictorial fashion—the movement of spirit: "For spirit is knowledge of self in a state of alienation of self; spirit is the being which is the process of retaining identity with itself in its otherness" (*ibid.*). It was as this very process of "mediating with its own self its transitions from one state or position to the opposite" (*P*, §18; *PM*, p. 80) or of being "in its otherness, . . . still one with itself" (*P*, §25; *PM*, p. 86), that Hegel also defined the concept of spirit in the Preface. This movement, which is represented in religion, remains, however, still external to the act of representing itself. In order to arrive at absolute knowledge of itself, the absolute spirit must therefore go over from the "form of a pictorial idea" (*PG*, p. 547; *PM*, p. 783) to that of the concept. It is only the conceiving that is wholly identical with the movement of the spirit and is the latter's self-cognition, in which it now evolves into a system of thought-determinations; as Hegel writes in the Preface: "Mind, which, when thus developed, knows itself to be mind, is *Science*" (*P*, §25; *PM*, p. 86). This science, the system of pure thought-determinations, is logic—and this shows that Hegel's concept of spirit, although it originally belongs to religion, has its roots in the tradition of *logos* philosophy. It is the perfectly logical character of the real which finds expression in the concept. This only becomes perfectly clear if we take a look ahead to the later systematic scheme of the *Encyclopaedia*, where the spirit's self-presentation in all areas of the real is of decisive importance. Although we are here confining ourselves in general to the *Phenomenology*, we shall now for once give indications in this direction, in order to get a better idea of the meaning of Hegel's much-debated concept of spirit. To the difference between the systematic views of the *Encyclopaedia* and those sketched out at the conclusion of the *Phenomenology*, we shall again briefly return.

One of the clearest accounts of the concept of spirit is to be found in the 1830 version of the *Encyclopaedia* (*Werke*, VII/2), in the Introduction to its third part, the *Philosophy of Mind* [Spirit]. We there read in the *Zusatz* to §385: "Mind is essentially only what it knows itself to be. At first it is only potentially mind; its becoming-for-itself makes it an actuality" (*HPM*, p. 21).

This simple statement has a manifold content. For one thing, the concept of mind designates an act, namely that of "apprehending" itself, and thus its nature, its own concept. And it is in this very apprehension that its self-actualization lies, i.e., the actualizing of its own concept.

The meaning of these simple statements will be correctly appreciated only if we bear in mind at the same time the underlying tendency of Hegel's entire scheme. For him, the *logos*—the "logical Idea"—permeates all that is (cf. *op. cit.*, §381, *Zusatz; HPM*, p. 8). The logical Idea is mind [or spirit] "in itself." It reveals itself in a *first* way through a "release" of the logical Idea into the "immediacy of external and particularized existence" (*ibid.*, §384, *Zusatz; HPM*, p. 18). This release is the becoming of Nature, which to that extent—just like the logical Idea—constitutes a "presupposition" of actual mind, mind for itself. "Actual mind . . . has external Nature for its proximate, and the logical Idea for its first, presupposition" (*ibid.*, §381, *Zusatz; HPM*, p. 8). But in its form Nature contradicts the concept of mind, which lies not at all in externality but in "inwardness" (*ibid.; HPM*, p. 9). For this very reason the "mind implicit, slumbering in Nature, overcomes . . . the externality, separateness and immediacy [of Nature]." It "thereby becomes mind which is reflected into itself and is for itself, self-conscious and awakened mind or mind as such" (*ibid.*, §384, *Zusatz; HPM*, pp. 18–19).

In the account given of consciousness in the *Phenomenology*, we did indeed see how its nature consists in counter-posing to itself an object, whose status (for it) is that of something merely given or present. If what confronts consciousness, or rather self-consciousness, is for its own part already "mind in itself," i.e., mind which conceals itself non-consciously in nature as much as it reveals itself, then it can be seen that consciousness, or rather self-consciousness as mind aware of itself, is able to apprehend itself in the object as something of its own kind. Through the onset of the movement in mind-in-itself, it becomes evident that the reality of what is present as a counterpart to self-consciousness consists, in fact, in its being "posited" by mind—and for that very reason it must also be so transformed as to correspond, fully and completely, to the concept of mind.

What the process consists in, therefore, is that mind or spirit, which takes back into its inwardness the externality of nature, sublates the latter into this, as into the "self-knowing, actual Idea" (ibid., §379, Zusatz; HPM, p. 5), or that it "idealizes" Nature. The most important determinacy of the concept of spirit is "ideality." The spirit as Idea sublates what is other to it and thereby reverts from this other back into itself.

The act of the spirit proves to be a differentiating and re-shaping of itself, and a leading back of its differentiation to the unity of its concept. This act is typical of the manner in which the thinking spirit of man knows itself as an "I." The I realizes itself as this ideality of the spirit, and authenticates this ideality in its relation to the manifold material confronting it. Through its representing activity the I—as finite spirit—posits "things . . . into its own interior space" (ibid., §381, Zusatz; HPM, p. 11). As thought, the I is spirit, "in the form of universality, of self-existent, actually free mind" (ibid.; HPM, p. 14); as the I, in thinking, grasps its material, the latter becomes "at the same time poisoned and transfigured by the universality [of the I]; it loses its isolated, independent existence and receives a spiritual one" (ibid.; HPM, p. 11). This takes place in particular through philosophical thinking, which brings about an idealization of things in that it recognizes the particular way in which the eternal Idea forming their common principle is presented in them. In philosophical thinking the spirit makes itself into the actual Idea in perfect apprehension of itself, and thus into absolute spirit. Thus in philosophical thinking the spirit attains to its concept. All external objectivity or "Nature," in which it has "alienated" itself, is sublated in subjectivity, in the Idea come to its own being-for-itself. This self-identity of the spirit, achieved out of this difference, testifies to its power of securing "in" the other a total independence of the other, of so "enduring" otherness that by sublation of the latter it proves in general to be the Idea reverting to itself out of its otherness, the self-differentiating which in its difference is with and for itself. The spirit attests its power of again finding itself in this contradiction, in this division, in the negative it has posited, and thus of again negating the latter. As such a power of "absolute negativity," the substance of spirit is "freedom," i.e., non-dependence on another, or self-relation to self. In this way the spirit engenders its own freedom, liberates itself from all forms of its being which do not correspond to its concepts, by transforming them into a reality appropriate to the concept of spirit.

This self-liberating act of the spirit is ultimately performed as a "self-revelation." In the other, the spirit reveals itself in its concept as spirit existing-in-itself or logical Idea, as the alienation of this in immediacy, as Nature, and as the self-conscious spirit existing-for-itself, which in its inwardness has made this immediacy of Nature conform to universality. This self-revelation comes to completion when every dualism between an independent Nature and spirit on the way to being-for-itself is again overcome; and is realized, therefore, as "absolute spirit," which reveals itself in infinitely creative fashion as the absolute unity of its existence in and for itself. In its absolute revelation this absolute spirit is "absolute truth." At the standpoint of absolute spirit, i.e., of art, religion, and philosophy, the spirit does not realize itself merely subjectively, nor does it apprehend itself merely as objective spirit, which is given in the external reality of its freedom, for instance in the state, in which it has developed to the point of positing itself as an ethical world; as absolute spirit, it has sublated all positedness in itself.

All finitudes are negated, and have been transformed into a moment of the infinite spirit.

We have here elucidated Hegel's concept of spirit by reference to the statements of the *Encyclopaedia* and its system; but it should not indeed go unmentioned, that although already in his own advertisement to the *Phenomenology* Hegel had announced the tripartite division of the system into Logic, Philosophy of Nature, and Philosophy of Mind, the conclusion of the work contains a different view of its constituent parts. Without entering here into discussion about the development of Hegel's conception of his system,[7] we may briefly refer to that conception at this point, since it once again throws light on the meaning of history—regarded as an educational history of absolute spirit—for the "Idea" of the Phenomenology. In the final sections of the *Phenomenology*, Hegel distinguishes the absolute self-containment of spirit and three modes of its externalization. The spirit, to which consciousness has attained in the final shape of the Phenomenology, namely absolute knowledge, presents itself initially in the pure "ether of its life" (*PG*, p. 562; *PM*, p. 805), that is, in the form of the concept. This presentation is the science of logic. But the spirit attains to the "highest freedom and security of its knowledge of itself" (*PG*, p. 563; *PM*, p. 806) only when it renounces this pure form of itself and presents itself in what seem to it the alien elements of consciousness, space and time or history; by which presentation it appropriates these elements to itself, idealizes them in the sense discussed above. The first externalization, that into consciousness, is nothing else but the sequence of shapes of consciousness presented in the *Phenomenology*: thus the *Phenomenology* now discloses itself as a necessary logical sequence. The second, the spirit's self-intuition in the element of space, is the philosophy of Nature. The third is the presentation of the spirit's becoming, i.e., its increasing self-knowledge in the temporal sequence of its shapes, i.e., in history. Hegel does not have in view here a philosophy of world-history, in the sense in which he later presented it, as a self-realizing of the objective spirit. His concern, rather, is with a presentation of the self-education of the absolute spirit in history. It involves a "conservation" of the cultural stages of the spirit in history "looked at from the side of their free existence appearing in the form of contingency" (*PG*, p. 564; *PM*, p. 808), i.e., from the side of history as a contingent temporal succession of cultural forms—and a conceiving of these historical shapes as stages in a necessary process of becoming on the part of absolute spirit. This conceiving, which transforms the contingent sequence of spiritual shapes into a necessary "organization," is again the Phenomenology of Spirit, insofar as it somehow "prepares"—in the manner already discussed—the "labor" the spirit has accomplished in world-history for the ushering of the natural consciousness into science. Whether Hegel here has in view the granting of autonomy to one side of the Phenomenology, in the form of a cultural history divorced from the task of ushering natural consciousness into science,[8] can be left undiscussed, as well as the difficult question of what is actually meant by saying that, according to Hegel, it is only the "conceived organization" of history *together* with the "conservation" of the historical shapes in their contingent mode of appearance, which constitutes "history conceived." [9] What matters for the one conception exhibited here of Hegel's system at the time he wrote the *Phenomenology* is this tripartite division of the spirit's externalization into consciousness, Nature, and conceived history.

But let us now return again to the becoming of absolute spirit, as it is viewed in the presentation of the *Phenomenology* —whose Idea and method are here our primary concern. This progress toward absolute or infinite spirit, and within this, to absolute knowledge, is now—as we have seen—presented by the *Phenomenology of Spirit* as a movement in which the spirit, in the *"element of positive immediate existence"* (P, §35; *PM*, p. 96), and that means as consciousness, becomes an other to itself, i.e., an object of its self, alienates itself and then sublates this otherness, returning back from this alienation into itself. The Phenomenology describes how the spirit evolves in the element of this opposition between knowing and objecthood, how it emerges in the mode of successive shapes of consciousness in its relation to the changing objectivity, the logical moments. The course of this development, in which consciousness relates to its moments, is the course of an "experience" undergone by consciousness.

Having rendered the concept of spirit more precise, we shall now try to demonstrate, under four headings, the extent to which the Phenomenology is at the same time both a science of the experience of consciousness and a science of spirit.

1. §17 of the Introduction presents an account of the *entire* Phenomenology of Spirit. It is described both as an "entire system of . . . the experience which *consciousness* has concerning itself" [10] and likewise ("or") as "the whole realm of the truth of *mind* [spirit]" (*PM*, p. 144). This implies that the subject of all experience is equally both consciousness and spirit, or more exactly, the spirit as consciousness; science (the system) has this experience for its object; as science of spirit it is the science of the experience of consciousness. In the Preface, this conception of an identity between science of spirit and science of experience is adhered to and actually rendered more explicit still. §36 of the Preface speaks, just as does §17 of the Introduction, of the Phenomenology as though it were a "system of the experience of spirit," and the science which presents this system is described in §36 as a "science of the *experience* through which consciousness passes" (*PM*, p. 96). The identity of science of experience and science of spirit could find no clearer expression than it does in the fact that in one and the same paragraph, in alternate sentences, the movement of the experience of *consciousness* and the movement of the experience of *spirit* are described as being of the same kind; the fact that the spirit referred to in this context is the spirit in the *"element of positive immediate existence"* (*P*, §35; *PM*, p. 96), the spirit as "appearing" (*P*, §38; *PM*, p. 97), does not contradict this. The Phenomenology of Spirit as a science that "makes its appearance" was also viewed in the Introduction (§4; *PM*, p. 134) as "appearing" (cf. above, pp. 24 f.).

2. §17 of the Introduction defines the particular nature of the

Phenomenology more exactly: in it "consciousness" in its various shapes is related to the logical moments. As the above-cited first sentence of §17 clearly shows, this too holds good of it both as a science which describes the "experience which consciousness has of itself," and also as one which constitutes the "whole realm of the truth of mind." Here again we may draw upon §36 of the Preface, which treats expressly of "consciousness," insofar as it designates the "immediate existence" of mind or spirit. Spirit in its primordial division into knowing and objecthood is spirit as subjective reference to itself, as reflection which has set up something external in opposition to itself; it knows this initial other only in the shape of something independent of itself. Both beginning and end of this movement are defined in the same fashion for consciousness and spirit alike. So far as the end is concerned, it is clearly stated that once the spirit has returned from its estrangement, the "abstract" or what is thought has become a "possession of consciousness."

3. Finally paragraph 17 also characterizes the two-stage goal both of the entire movement of experience and also of the presentation of this movement, i e., of the Phenomenology as a science of experience and also of spirit. For the natural consciousness as phenomenal knowledge, the goal lies simply in the fact that it has consumed its naturalness and is no longer hampered with what is foreign to it; for the presentation of this same movement the goal lies in the fact that as presentation of experience in Books A, B and C, it attains, by way of the stages of consciousness, self-consciousness, reason, spirit, and religion, to the final stage of "absolute knowledge." The first phase of this goal is located, for experiencing consciousness, at the point where "appearance" becomes equivalent to its essence, though without consciousness having already "grasped this its own essence." It coincides with the first phase of the goal of presentation, which is reached at the point where the "science proper of mind" begins, i.e., with section VI of the text. The final goal for experiencing consciousness comes when it "grasps this its own essence"; this final goal coincides with that of the

presentation of "absolute knowledge." What this means is that presentation refers up to the end to the *experience* of consciousness as it presses forward to its true existence. Both as an inauthentic and an authentic science of *spirit* (and also as a presentation of the spirit *qua* absolute knowledge), the Phenomenology of Spirit, as a science related to *experience,* is a science of the experience of consciousness.

4. That conversely, the Phenomenology seeks from the outset to be a science of spirit, can be confirmed from two other passages of the text; in the first place, from that in which we are told—already early in the presentation of self-consciousness: "With this we already have before us the notion [concept] of *Mind* or *Spirit*" (*PG,* p. 140; *PM,* p. 227). The most important confirmation, however, is the passage where the science of spirit begins for the philosopher. At the point where spirit discerns that it is itself "self-supporting absolutely real ultimate being" (*PG,* p. 314; *PM,* p. 459), it is expressly declared that all previous shapes of consciousness were "abstractions" of the spirit, modes in which the spirit was analyzing itself, as into its "moments." It is thereupon expressly stated that the "isolating" of such moments had spirit itself for its *"presupposition"* and *"subsistence."*

Our conception of the identity of science of experience and science of spirit does not contradict the assuredly correct view [11] that many basic concepts of the *Phenomenology* have been altered—in a way thoroughly consistent with the development of the presentation—and that the method as a process of examining consciousness is valid only so long as the latter is experientially oriented toward a "given" object, and has not yet discerned itself to be a spiritual being.

Having cleared up the significance of spirit in the approach of the Phenomenology, and the sense in which the latter is both science of experience and science of spirit, let us return to the question posed at the outset of this chapter. What method does the Phenomenology employ to resolve its two appointed tasks, and what concept of knowledge is presupposed in doing so?

2. The Method according to the Introduction

1. Let us remind ourselves that, for Hegel, consciousness constitutes the "immediate existence" of spirit (*P*, §§35, 36; *PM*, p. 96), whereas the self-mediating spirit is consciousness as the movement of "becoming other to itself," which at the same time proceeds to "transcend this otherness" (*P*, §36; *PM*, p. 96). In order that the spirit *qua* consciousness may become other to itself, it must realize the "negativity" (cf. above, pp. 17 f.) peculiar to the latter, whereby there arises a dissimilarity of two opposing sides, of which the one is knowledge, and the other the "objectivity . . . negative of . . . knowing" (*ibid.*). On the other hand, if spirit wishes to "sublate" this otherness, the opposing sides must be set to finding their way back to a new identity. This movement of reuniting the sides posited as unlike gives rise to the translucency, that transparency of all that is, in which the Greeks saw the dominion of spirit, or *nous*.

Consciousness therefore distinguishes something from itself, and that which is so distinguished retains a reference to it. It is "for consciousness"—"for it"; it has a being that exists for consciousness. The "being of something for consciousness," or "being for another," is realized as a "referring." This referring is knowledge. Knowledge is able to reunite itself with the side opposed to it in various ways; in its perfected shape this takes place as a special act of closing up this primordial cleavage; this is knowledge as absolute conception, by which the subject brings the opposing side of objectivity into identity with the self realizing itself as knowledge, or with subjectivity—through the latter. If we now consider the structure of knowledge in the shape given to it in modern philosophy by Descartes, we find that consciousness, *qua* knowing subject, poses to itself an opposite or object distinct from itself. If we look at it the other way round, the object so posed, or the content of representation, stands in reference to consciousness, has "being" for consciousness, belongs to representative cognition as a known object or content. But at the same time,

2. "What is related to knowledge is likewise distinguished from it, and posited as also *existing* outside this relation" (*I*, §10; *PM*, p. 139). An "objectivity" (*P*, §36; *PM*, p. 96) exists in the realm of consciousness in a respect quite different from that previously referred to. It likewise ranks as something opposed to knowledge, and does so, indeed, as though it had nothing whatever to do with consciousness and its knowing. For knowing it ranks as existing "in itself" or "on its own." This characterization can have two meanings: in the first place, that the object has for consciousness the ontological status of subsisting like a thing, a being ranking as utterly alien to any sort of thought and lying wholly outside this. The movement of the Phenomenology will show, indeed, that the modes of cognition which ascribe this character of subsistence to the object are erroneous, and that the "object" is by no means thing-like and alien to thought, but rather belongs to thought and is moved thereby and is thus not thing-like at all.

In the second and much more important sense of "being in itself," objectivity is construed as a "standard" independent of cognition and determining the latter. For traditional metaphysics, eternally subsistent essence, or essential "being," had for centuries provided the standard for knowledge, for both had the status of being "true." As we have already gathered from Hegel's sketch of the history of culture, this truth took shape quite early in the form of "abbreviations," which had reduced reality to its basic determinations, and thus already "canceled" it as existing outside thought (*P*, §29; *PM*, p. 91). These abbreviations are thought-determinations or categories; in their entirety they constituted the "truth" of what is, which they thus made merely "true." At the same time, however, they had made knowledge of such "being" into "true knowledge." Depending on whether the traditional metaphysics viewed the matter in a "Platonic" or an "Aristotelian" fashion, this truth or standard was taken to lie "beyond" the existent, or to dwell "in" it, determining it concretely from within.

For modern philosophy since Kant, the truth or standard has lain in the rules of knowledge, or categories, i.e., in essentialities together comprising the total structure of a "form," which ultimately constitutes the essence, or subjectivity, of the self. So far as the self, through its form, at the same time also gives logical shape to the presented material or content—the object—this form is rightly also called "objectivity." The form, as it articulates itself in its various kinds of categories and essentialities, is thus at the same time both subjectivity and objectivity. At the beginning of the modern development, however, it was not yet fully recognized that, and how, the essence of truth is connected with the nature of the subject and its formative activity in cognition. This essence was taken to be posited outside consciousness, to be the side which, *qua* "in itself," constituted "truth." It is in this form that the Introduction takes up "truth." As such it is the standard whereby consciousness measures whether the object or content cognitively presented by it is a true one (and to that extent the essence or "being"), and whether its knowledge is true. To this we shall return. But first it must be noted that consciousness, when it represents to itself an object as known content, can only know it as a "true" one, if at the same time its objecthood, i.e., its form or truth, is present to view.

In the Introduction, Hegel gave these truth-articulating thought-determinations the name of "moments" (§17; *PM,* p. 144); together they constitute the "whole realm of . . . truth." In the *Phenomenology,* however, these moments do not figure— as they do in the *Logic*—as "abstract pure moments," but in such a way as to stand in a relationship to consciousness: they are "for consciousness" or "as consciousness itself appears in its relation to them" (*ibid.; PM,* pp. 144–45). Thus, to the consciousness of perception—to name an example—(Section A, ch. II), the categories of being-for-self and being-for-another do not appear in their purely logical form, but as aspects of things or of their properties. In the apprehension of properties, for example, as indifferent to one another, i.e., as coexisting in the unity of a thing without "affecting" each other, we find the category of pure self-relation or being-for-self. If, on the other hand, either properties or things are viewed as distinct, in the sense of excluding one another, this is the manner in which the category of being-for-another, or the—in this case negative—relation to another, appears to a consciousness engaged in experience.

It is true even for logic—and Hegel had already said as much in the *Jena Logic*—that a single determination, viewed merely in isolation, is false. Every individual determination has already vested its meaning in other determinations which pertain to it. This "concreteness" holds good to a still greater extent, and in another way, for the various shapes of consciousness. For them, truth is mostly an indistinct correlation of determinations, Together they constitute for consciousness the structure of the currently prevailing "in-itself."

This paragraph confirms, at all events, that there are thought-determinations (or moments) which constitute truth "for itself." Moreover, it may also serve to prevent an otherwise natural misunderstanding which could easily result from Hegel's employment of the term "object." When Hegel speaks in the Introduction of an "object," then—depending on the context—this may mean on the one hand the "represented content" which "exists for consciousness" through its relating or knowing, while on the other hand this title may refer to the "truth," form, or "objectivity," which renders both the known object and the knowing of it true.

That Hegel omitted, in the Introduction, to distinguish in this way between objectivity and object, should perhaps make it apparent how the moments emerge in the Phenomenology as "shapes of consciousness." They do not so appear that consciousness itself is able to make a separation between the represented object (content) and the collective structure of an objectivity, or truth. To put it all-too-simply, consciousness, in its naïve modes, behaves in an "Aristotelian" fashion; for it, the form (objectivity) "resides" in the object (content). More exactly, it is simply not aware of any such distinction. But not only does it fail to abstract the "form" from the "formed"; it is also unaware that, and how, this form, this entire structure of thought-determinations appearing as truth, belongs "in" consciousness; for which reason, indeed, it takes them to be posited in the definition of the *"per se"* (or "in-itself"). That such determinations are really thought-determinations of the self must first result, for consciousness, from the further determination of the shapes of consciousness. More precisely, it must turn out that these thought-determinations are themselves "moments of the concept." The movement of self-examination which takes place in the light of these moments will demonstrate, in fact, that as "truths" of the self, and thus ultimately of the concept, they belong to the latter, not only "in themselves," nor even merely "for themselves," but are valid "in and for themselves." It will appear to consciousness that the side of truth, and the side of knowing itself, form a unity or identity, the identity of an object (or substance) and a subject that overlaps its object.

3. For the method of the Phenomenology, as the Introduction presents it, the foregoing explanations yield the following: since one side of consciousness is the total structure of the objectivity negative to knowledge, and since this objectivity provides the standard, it follows that consciousness "furnishes its own criterion in itself" (*I*, §12; *PM*, p. 140).[12] Within itself it can examine—in its various shapes—whether that in the represented object (content) which ranks for it as the "true," the essence or essentially existent, is known in a manner corresponding to this truth, and this through a knowledge which guarantees that it has apprehended its object adequately as a true one. Consciousness is able to examine in this fashion, because as such it is always both consciousness of "what is true to it"—and thus of the total structure of thought-determinations constituting the truth—and "consciousness of its knowledge thereof." Both consciousness of the true and consciousness of knowing the truth are *"for the same* consciousness," which can therefore be defined in its essential structure as the "comparison" of these two sides (*I*, §13; *PM*, p. 141). But consciousness is also knowledge of an object that it knows to be true, and can therefore measure or compare by this standard. To state this in terms of an example from the chapter on perception: Consciousness knows its object, say a salt crystal, as a thing that is the bearer of properties.

The perceiving consciousness has thereby set up a standard prefiguring for the known content a total structure of determinations, and thus imposes a series of requirements upon knowledge. That the salt should be a thing, signifies, for example, that it has to be apprehended as something distinct from other things, i.e., as an exclusive "one"; and again, that in spite of the differences presented by its properties—of being tart, cubical, white, etc.—it must constitute, *qua* thing, the unity of a "selfsameness." The properties, also, which are perceived in the salt crystal, must satisfy various preconditions: they have to be specific and distinct from one another, but at the same time must be indifferent to one another, so as to be able to coexist in the thing. Hence the standard applied by consciousness contains "prescriptions" both for knowledge and for the object. Their collective significance for the structure of consciousness is that this consciousness is on the one hand a comparison of form with knowledge (representing), and on the other, a comparison of form with the represented object (content). It is in this fashion that consciousness consists in an act of self-examination.

It is now more clearly apparent why phenomenal knowledge is able to take over these two tasks of phenomenology, and why the phenomenologist is able to delegate them and—so it seems at first sight, anyway—to confine himself "solely to look[ing] on" (*I*, §13; *PM*, p. 141). To be sure, the presentation—as we particularly stressed at the outset of our discussion—aims at being an "inquiry"; it seeks to undertake an "examination into the reality of knowing" (*I*, §9; *PM*, p. 139), to deal with the "truth of knowledge" (*I*, §11; *PM*, p. 140). But if the phenomenal knowledge which the presentation takes along with it is so structured as to operate essentially as a comparison or examination, then "we"—the phenomenologists—have no need to do this ourselves.

We now see more clearly that, in virtue of its own nature, "phenomenal knowledge" furnishes the "standard," the "objectivity," the truth appearing as a totality of moments or thought-determinations. We have likewise already discerned that knowing or conceiving (the concept for itself), and its object, are moments of a consciousness, and also that "being-for-another" and "being-in-itself" are its determinations. If all this automatically belongs to the nature of self-consciousness—and hence to that of phenomenal knowledge—why should there then be any need of a phenomenologist coming in from outside? On the contrary, we even seem called upon to leave "*our* fancies and thoughts" aside "in the inquiry"; for in this way we are much better able to arrive at "the subject [of phenomenal knowledge] as it actually is *in itself* and *for itself*" (*I*, §12; *PM*, p. 141).[13] In contrast to the natural consciousness of Hegel's day, which, as an "understanding" consciousness, is to be persuaded that it could itself take the road of phenomenal knowledge, the phenomenologist therefore finds himself in the happy position, for the persuasiveness of the examination, of letting consciousness examine itself—by its own standards. Precisely because phenomenological science has reduced itself to "appearance" (cf. above, p. 25) and viewed itself as involved in the process of the becoming of the whole, and because it has not yet "carried out" science proper "in all the length and breadth of its truth" (*I*, §4; *PM*, p. 134),[14] it has not yet been able in any way to "justify" its own standard. If it were to try to apply an unjustified standard to the contemporary natural consciousness, the latter "would not necessarily have to recognize" this. (*I*, §§9 and 11; *PM*, pp. 139, 140).

4. If, therefore, it lies in the nature of phenomenal knowledge to be able to compare and examine for itself, then in each and every shape it can subject its claim to truth to critical examination. In the course of this self-examination it will measure both the side of the knowing self, and that of the presented content, by the "moment" or form of truth determining the shape in question; it will discover all the contradictions existing between this form and knowledge, on the one hand, and the represented object (content) on the other and dispose of them step by step. The perceptual consciousness discovers, for example, that there is a contradiction between the *standard* it applies to things and its knowledge of them, e.g., the determination of selfsameness, and the thing itself or its own apprehension thereof;

71

the thing appears to it as internally contradictory—on the one hand as subsisting for itself, or independent, and on the other as determined by its relation to something else, as non-independent or a mere "relation" (*PG,* p. 99; *PM,* p. 174). The same contrariety is evinced in its apprehension, which not only wavers between these two aspects of the thing, but also between opposing views of the two "sides" of perception, consciousness and the thing; on the one hand it declares the thing to be simple, and its differences—e.g., the whiteness or cubicalness of the salt—to belong to the side of the perceptual consciousness or its various sense-perceptions; then the thing in turn strikes it as a mere conglomeration of differences, which are first unified in consciousness. Hence—as emerges from the self-examination of perception—the opposition between thing and modes of apprehension does not conform to their standard: selfsameness. This means, then, with regard to experience in general, that if it emerges from such comparison that form, on the one hand, and knowledge or represented object (content) on the other, fail to correspond, then such a result of self-examination will "compel" phenomenal knowledge to alter its knowing and make it fit the form. Phenomenal knowledge took the view, indeed, that the side of the object constituting its "subsistence," like that of the truth which determines it as "true," must be wholly independent of cognition, and therefore *"per se"* (or "in itself"). But it is obliged to recognize that "in the alteration of the knowledge, the object itself also, in point of fact, is altered" (*I,* §13; *PM,* p. 142).[15] With the altering of its knowledge, the objectivity of the object has more or less unwittingly changed for it as well: "for the knowledge which existed was essentially a knowledge of the object [objectivity]; with change in the knowledge, the object also becomes different, since it belonged essentially to this knowledge" (*ibid.*).[16] This, as we emphasized, is the decisive insight to which phenomenal knowledge repeatedly attains at each stage of its shaping: namely that the thought-determinations or forms constituting objectivity are not only forms of an object separate from knowledge, but are

72

also forms of knowledge, and to that extent belong to knowledge or the self. At each stage it therefore recognizes in provisional fashion that the thought-determinations are those of the self viewed as concept. As the Introduction puts it: ". . . consciousness comes to find that what formerly to it was the essence is not what is *per se*" or was "only *per se for consciousness.*" [17] Phenomenal knowledge has to recognize in each case that what served it as the standard of examination does not itself "hold out" (*ibid.*) [18] in its *per se* character, precisely because "what at first appeared as object is reduced . . . [for] consciousness, to a knowledge of it, and the *per se* becomes a being-for-consciousness of the *per se*" (*I*, §15; *PM*, p. 144 [adapted]).[19] This implies, therefore, that "the standard for examining is altered when that, whose criterion this standard was to be, does not hold its ground in the course of the examination; and the examination is not only an examination of knowledge, but also of the criterion used in the process" (*I*, §13; *PM*, p. 142).[20]

We must go on to ask: In what way does self-consciousness determine itself from one shape to the next? How does it advance from the validity of an old true object to that of a new true object? Hegel's answer to this question is that it gets there by way of "experience." Experience in its proper sense he defines as "this dialectic process which consciousness executes on itself—on its knowledge as well as on its object—in the sense that out of it the new and true object arises . . ." (*I*, §14; *PM*, p. 142).[21] Let us attempt to characterize this experience more fully.

Consciousness must have undergone the movement of self-examination already described. It must have measured both the side of its knowledge, and that of the objectively represented content, by the standard hitherto prevailing for it, namely truth—the form or total structure of objectivity. In so doing, it must have discovered the contradictions between the form, on the one hand, and knowledge and the known content on the other; and it must have worked out these contradictions until the truth in them it hitherto accepted has been dissolved. At the end of this process of examination, it must have arrived at an "insight into the untruth" of its previous viewpoint, and seen that there is "nothing" in the truth prevailing till now.

According to the passage cited, however, experience includes, in addition to the examination-process, the apprehension by phenomenal knowledge of a "new and true object." This latter seems for it immediately to take the place of the old one; it "finds" it "casually and externally" (*I*, §15; *PM*, p. 143); [22] in this sense the new object "arises" (or "emerges") for it, so to speak (*I*, §14; *PM*, p. 142). It must be stressed that it is not part of the "experience" of phenomenal knowledge to recognize and perceive as one movement the connection between the double process of examination leading to the "nothing" of the old object, and the apprehension of the new and true one; nor does it recognize this movement to be "dialectical" in character. As we shall soon see, it is only the phenomenologist who recognizes it as such. The naïveté which besets the experience of phenomenal knowledge is precisely that it has no inkling at all of any connection between the old and the new object, nor of the essential structure of this connection.

The experience of phenomenal knowledge does, however, seem to include something else. At the end of the examination it recognizes that the old object, the truth, is in no way "also *existing* outside this relation" (*I*, §10; *PM*, p. 139) [23] to consciousness or knowledge. It becomes aware that, through this examination, "What at first appeared as object is reduced . . . to a knowledge of it, and the *per se* becomes a being-for-consciousness of the *per se*" (*I*, §15; *PM*, p. 144 [adapted]. See n. 19 above). Now although this insight may be part of its "experience," phenomenal knowledge still fails to draw any conclusions from it. It might have arrived at the insight that it now has "two objects," the one being the first *per se* (or "in-itself"), and the other the being-for-consciousness of this *per se*. But this view it immediately rejects, since the fact that the old object has turned into a "being-for-consciousness" of the *per se* tells it that the old object is no longer any object at all, in the sense of a self-subsistent truth, but

74

merely a "reflection of consciousness into itself," merely the "idea . . . of its knowledge of that first object" (cf. *I*, §14; *PM*, pp. 142–43). And hence phenomenal knowledge persists in the belief that the old object has ceased to be a standard and is to be treated as if it were nothing. It must be cast into the "abysmal void" (*I*, §7; *PM*, p. 137). Phenomenal knowledge is here persuaded that it did not undergo this experience because the old object changed in the course of examination, but because it has itself discovered the new object. In the light of the new truth it thinks it has done away with the old object as nothing; it is simply the discovery of the new object which appears to it as "experience" (cf. *I*, §14; *PM*, pp. 142–43).

It therefore emerges that although phenomenal knowledge keeps determining itself through "experience," from one shape to another, it perceives no connection between the preceding object and the following one. That, and how, a "transition" is effected from one object to the next, is simply not observable to phenomenal knowledge. Thus it also appears to be unaware in its experience that it is on a "road" leading to a quite specific goal, namely absolute knowledge. But it is in fact taking this road, and is therefore doubtlessly doing so on the basis of its "experience." Could it be that phenomenal knowledge is essentially incapable of discerning what is actually implicit in its experience? At this point it appears that "we"— the phenomenologists—have a role to play which goes beyond anything so far described. This role, we saw, consisted in carrying phenomenal knowledge with us along the road of presentation—although phenomenal knowledge is able, indeed, to conduct its self-examination without any reference to the phenomenologist's standards, and, proceeding from one shape to another, can arrive at that of absolute knowledge, which constitutes the "concept of knowledge." Up to now it has seemed as though phenomenal knowledge could independently fulfill both the tasks of phenomenology (see above, pp. 24 f.). So much was inherent in its principle, according to which self-consciousness is its "concept for itself." To be sure, our distinction between "natural consciousness as such" and "phenomenal knowledge" had already alerted us to one fact, namely that consciousness will only evolve this principle if it is carried along by the presentation and compelled by it into "despair" and into the method of self-realizing skepticism. Without this, it would persist *qua* "natural consciousness as such," in some particular shape and never press on to absolute knowledge. From these considerations it was already evident that in realizing the principle of self-consciousness the scientist plays a role. But a further aspect of this role has also come to our notice. We saw it in the fact that the phenomenologist discerns the naïveté of phenomenal knowledge, which fails to recognize what really constitutes and brings about its own experience. For our problem concerning the "Idea" of the Phenomenology it is important to define more closely this aspect of the phenomenologist's role, and to set forth not only those respects in which he has a more accurate view of the structure of phenomenal knowledge's experience, but also the consequences that result for the course of the Phenomenology as a whole.

NOTES

1. ". . . what remains for us . . . . is simply the pure act of *observation*" (*D*, p. 21).

2. ". . . consciousness is for itself its own *Concept* . . ." (*D*, p. 17).

3. ". . . exist in consciousness" (*D*, p. 19).

4. On the origins of the concept of "objective spirit," cf. M. Riedel, "Objectiver Geist und praktische Philosophie," in *Studien zu Hegels Rechtsphilosophie*, Frankfurt 1969, pp. 11–41.

5. J. Hyppolite, *Genèse et Structure de la Phénoménologie de l'Esprit*, Paris 1946, II, p. 312.

6. ". . . essence which is in and for itself . . ." (Tr.).

7. Cf. H. Kimmerle, "Dokumente zu Hegels Jenaer Dozententätigkeit (1801–1807)," in *Hegel-Studien*, Bonn 1967, pp. 22–29, and H. F. Fulda, *op. cit.*, pp. 93 ff.

8. This is pointed out by H. F. Fulda, *op. cit.*, p. 266. As was already

observed earlier, however, the proof that a history of education is necessary as an independent "philosophical discipline" (*ibid.*, p. 221) can be established only on the basis of the conception of the encyclopaedic system. From the final section of the *Phenomenology* under discussion at present, it is, at all events, impossible to extract any direct evidence that the conceiving of history as an "organization" of the educational stages of absolute spirit should be reserved to any other discipline than that of the "science of phenomenal knowledge."

9. Even the attempted solution by H. F. Fulda (*op. cit.*, p. 103) has still not explained this difficulty satisfactorily.

10. "The experience which consciousness makes of itself . . ." (*D*, p. 26).

11. Cf. O. Pöggeler, "Zur Deutung . . . ," *op. cit.*, p. 289.

12. ". . . consciousness provides itself with its own standard . . ." (*D*, p. 20).

13. ". . . *our* preconceived ideas and thoughts during this investigation . . . . the subject matter as it is *in* and *for itself*" (*D*, p. 21).

14. ". . . in its fully realized and propagated truth . . ." (*D*, p. 12).

15. "In the alteration of the knowledge, however, the object itself becomes to consciousness something which has in fact been altered as well" (*D*, p. 22).

16. ". . . the object also becomes an other, since it was an essential part of this knowledge" (*D*, p. 22).

17. "Hence it comes to pass for consciousness that what had been to it the *in-itself* is not in itself, or, what was *in itself* was so only *f o r c o n - s c i o u s n e s s*" (*D*, p. 22).

18. ". . . fails to endure the course of the examination" (*D*, p. 23).

19. ". . . sinks to the level of being to consciousness a knowledge of the object, and when the *in-itself becomes a being-for-consciousness of the in-itself . . .*" (*D*, p. 25).

20. ". . . the standard of the examination is changed if that whose standard it was supposed to be fails to endure the course of the examination. Thus the examination is not only an examination of knowledge, but also of the standard used in the examination itself" (*D*, pp. 22–23).

21. "This *dialectical* movement, which consciousness exercises on its self . . . . *in so far as the new, true object emerges to consciousness . . .*" (*D*, p. 23).

22. ". . . we . . . discover [it] in a manner quite accidental and extraneous . . ." (*D*, p. 24).

23. ". . . posited as *existing* outside this relationship too" (*D*, p. 19).

VI

The Role of the Phenomenologist and the Genesis of the Concept of Science

TOWARD THE END of the Introduction there is talk of "our contribution"—i.e., that of the phenomenologist—which "does not exist for the consciousness we contemplate and consider" (*I*, §15; *PM*, p. 143). This contribution of ours—so we learn—is concerned with the contemplation of a "circumstance" which is only "for us." What does Hegel mean here by this "circumstance"? It refers to that insight belonging to the experience of phenomenal knowledge—already noted earlier—that in consequence of its self-examination the "*per se*" (or "in-itself") of the old object becomes a "being-for-consciousness of the *per se*." In this very circumstance—this experience of phenomenal knowledge—there lies for the phenomenologist a movement constituting the connection between experience of the "nothingness" of the old object and apprehension of the "new true object," a movement whose character is a "dialectical" one.

What does "dialectical" mean? This very difficult question can be answered here only in a very simplistic fashion. Fundamentally, a dialectical movement is one in which a positing—an initially unmediated, immediate position, a thesis—is negated or "sublated" (*tollere*) in its immediacy (in the sense of being removed), in that the sense-contents already implicit in this thesis are uncovered in their contradictoriness and posited as antitheses, and the contradictions, "pushed to extremes," negate themselves as such and are sublated to a result, a synthesis, "come about" from these sense-contents. The result of such a dialectical movement therefore consists in maintaining the opposites in a new unity (*conservare*) and raising them to it (*elevare*). Now how can the connection between the outcome of phenomenal knowledge's self-examination, i.e., its experience of the nothingness of the old object and of the emergence of the new, be regarded as a movement having a dialectical character? When a new shape begins to make its appearance, phenomenal knowledge posits its object, truth, as "in-itself"; this is the thesis. The examination itself, which uncovers the contradictions between truth (form) and knowledge on the one hand, and the presented object (content) on the other, is a movement of reflection constituting the antithesis. Whereas, for the consciousness of phenomenal knowledge, the experience ends in this antithesis, the phenomenologist observes that it continues. It goes on, indeed, to that point where, in the view of phenomenal knowledge, a completely new experiential process occurs: the "emergence" of the new true object. This very emergence appears to the phenomenologist as a "coming-to-be" or "becoming" arising out of this antithetical movement. It is the "result" or synthesis in which these discovered contradictions sublate themselves into the new true object. To be sure, the phenomenologist concurs with phenomenal knowledge in seeing this result as a "nothing," although one that is "determined" by the whole movement preceding it—a "determinate nothing" that he need only view positively in order to recognize it as the "principle" that has emerged, for him, out of the whole preceding movement (cf. *PG*, pp. 89 f.; *PM*, pp. 163 f.). This contemplation of the phenomenologist therefore discloses that the new object has "become" simply and solely through the fact that phenomenal consciousness has addressed itself to the old object, measured by this truth its current knowledge and the content presented, and uncovered the contradictions resulting from this comparison. He sees that with these movements of thought phenomenal knowledge is reflecting on the old object, is turning to it, that—as Hegel writes—through these reflections deriving from a *"turnabout of consciousness"* the *"new* object" has arisen. This means that the new object is really the old one, albeit with the difference that the new contains the "experience" gained of the old (*I*, §14; *PM*, p. 143), namely the experience of the "nothingness of the first" object (*ibid*.)., In short, the change in the determinations of the object from being *"per se"* ("in-itself") to a "being-for-consciousness of the *per se*" ("in-itself") signifies, for the phenomenologist, that the new object has come into being through the critical reflection of phenomenal knowledge, and thus through its own experience of the old object.

It cannot, however, be sufficiently emphasized that this contemplation of the emergence of the new object is not in fact known to phenomenal knowledge, although it constitutes the result of its own experience, properly understood. It is only for the phenomenologist that the new principle emerges in each case from the preceding critical reflection of phenomenal knowledge. As he sees it, this dialectical movement of experience on the part of phenomenal knowledge goes on "so to say, behind its back" (*I*, §15; *PM*, p. 144). This is the case, although it is simply and solely phenomenal knowledge which carries out this movement, and hence Hegel also expressly declares that "the *content* of what we see arising, exists *for it*," for the "consciousness engaged in the experience itself" (*ibid*.). Thus sense-certainty, for example (*PG*, pp. 89 ff.; *PM*, pp. 163 ff.), the first stage of phenomenal knowledge, becomes perception, in that consciousness goes over from the appearance of a sensory item, of which nothing more can be known than that it is a "this" present "here" and "now," to a knowing of things with determinate properties —such as, in Hegel's example, a salt crystal that is white, tart, cubical, etc. But it is only the philosopher who recognizes that consciousness *must* go over from the "this" to the "thing," or from sense-certainty to perception. For him, the "form" of the thing, to be universal or knowable as universal, is the necessary result of the experience of sense-certainty, which has been compelled to posit, and negate, the sensory item, and to reassemble it into a unity of many items. For if this movement is viewed, not merely negatively—as proof that the standard of sensory unity is untenable—but positively, then it is nothing else but the bringing forth of a universal. The universal of perception is, in fact—as Hegel says—the sensory content with the moment of negation, i.e., the determinate content, which distinguishes itself from any other: the salt is determined as white and not black, cubical and not flat. But this fact, however, that the principle of perception emerges from the negation of the principle of sense-certainty—the result of the experience, according to Hegel, is "a determinate nothing, a nothing with a certain content, viz. the This" (*PG*, p. 90; *PM*, p. 163)—is not recognized by the experiencing consciousness, but only by the philosopher. The phenomenologist thus uncovers this one side of the experience of phenomenal knowledge in its full significance, namely that—in virtue of its conceptual nature—it is able to carry out a dialectical movement, and that it is the latter which moves it on from one shape to another.

Let us make it yet clearer to ourselves what the phenomenologist discovers. He uncovers a structure which holds for any one of the shapes, and more importantly still, which constitutes their connection. For to say that in each case the new object—and the shape it determines—is nothing else but the "experience gained" from the preceding object (in its previous shape of consciousness), is to say in fact that these experiences together form a chain. By means of it, every new experience lines up to the one before it, and by this again to the one before that, and so back to the beginning of experience. Thus it is also the case, conversely, that the beginning, the first dialectical movement in this history of experiences, is sublated in the final shape and its object. Hence the latter is indeed the "result" of all the preceding experiences. And in this very fact we also find an expression of the meaning we commonly attach to the word "experience." We speak of our experience as "growing," and call a man experienced only if he "has learned from his experience" and is one for whom this experience has not disappeared through forgetting, but has grown in course of time and increasingly enriched itself.

The phenomenologist therefore discovers that it is part of the conceptual nature of self-consciousness to grow in this sense through "experiences." That this does not in fact refer to a man's individual self-consciousness, is a point already stressed in our introductory remarks.

The growth and enrichment does not, however, continue *ad infinitum;* the very fact that there is a "final" shape, having the character of a result of all that has gone before, implies a "closed" and not an open mode of growth. It cannot be too plainly emphasized that, for Hegel, the dialectical movement of the concept is a "teleological" one. Among the basic Aristotelian concepts, Hegel's whole conception is particularly guided by the concept of *telos* deriving from Aristotle's theory of substance, and this in the quite specific meanings which this concept has acquired through its translation into the *causa finalis* (cf. *P*, §§18 and 22; *PM*, pp. 80–81, 83). The end, in the sense of the "attained goal" and "fulfilled purpose," determines the beginning backward, "from the end," and with it all the stages of development of a process leading up to it. The goal as a cause effects the emergence of the form already implicit at the outset and in all stages and presupposed as a real possibility, or causes it to become increasingly "actual." In this way the end, as the highest, draws up the beginning and all the stages of development, the lower phases, toward itself. And the beginning, the presupposed conditions and developments, push forward accordingly in purposeful fashion to completion, to their purposive, fully realized goal. The pull of the *telos* and the push of the beginning toward it form the two sides of a final nexus, a thoroughly defined, self-enclosed circuit. Within this circuit there emerge the organs suitable for the realization of the purpose. The purpose organizes itself by means of them into its own organization.

If the self, or concept—which is ultimately reason—is viewed teleologically, its movement presents this same "unrest" whereby it stimulates the "purpose" inherent in its beginning—the "undisturbed" which "is self-moving" (*P*, §22; *PM*, p. 83)—to bring forth the "true" (*P*, §§18, 37; *PM*, pp. 80, 97), i.e., the concept in

82

the form of absolute knowledge. The "result" of this movement is the "realized" purpose. The self or concept, reverting from purpose (result) to purpose (beginning), as the "returned upon itself" (cf. *P*, §22 and *PG*, pp. 559, 563; *PM*, pp. 84, 802, 807) is "purposive activity" (*P*, §22; *PM*, p. 83), a "process of its own becoming, the circle which presupposes its end as its purpose, and has its end for its beginning [and] becomes concrete and actual only by being carried out, and by the end it involves" (*P*, §18; *PM*, p. 81).

In adherence to Kant's doctrine of method, the young Fichte, in an early publication ("On the Concept of the *Wissenschafts-lehre*"), had defined as "system" the mode and manner in which the self, concept, or reason, reverting teleologically into itself, becomes organized and thereby produces truth. For Hegel, too, the process occurring as experience organizes itself, in this sense, into an "entire system" (*I*, §17, cf. *P*, §38; *PM*, pp. 144, 97).

The self-enclosedness of a system which returns into itself guarantees that the shapes of phenomenal knowledge which attain to presentation are assembled in "complete" fashion (*I*, §7; *PM*, p. 137), and make their appearance in an inherently necessary succession, so that within the whole movement each one takes up a perfectly definite place.

In this way the phenomenologist makes it evident that the concept does not exhaust itself—as it does, say, in Kant—in an a priori apperception of the other. Above and beyond Kant's apperception, the concept as presented in the Phenomenology—directed towards the "true" in dialectical movements of experience, constantly growing, and completing itself in the *telos* of absolute truth—is able to produce the shape of a system. We saw the particular historicity of this movement in the fact that through it the natural consciousness works off its naturalness, so that—as the true—it becomes an absolute consciousness freed from any sort of "givenness." Through the presentation of this movement, the phenomenologist's observation demonstrates that phenomenal knowledge is capable of "being taken along" by his presentation on the road to this unfolding of the movement inherent within it. But how does this serve to define the role of the phenomenologist himself?

The Introduction (§15; *PM*, p. 143) has defined the role of the phenomenologist's "contemplation" only in the following respect: if "we" observe the "result-character" of the movement of experience stemming from the "turnabout of consciousness," the "emergence" of the new object from the old, we recognize the "necessity" whereby each "transition" is made from one object to the next. Through this insight, a "moment of being *per se* or of being for us" enters into the movement of consciousness, "which is not expressly for the consciousness which is engaged in experience itself." Thus here a "role" is expressly assigned to the phenomenologist. We, the phenomenologists, should pay attention to the necessity of the movement, for this is what makes it legitimate to describe even the presentation of the experience of consciousness—the road which first leads to science proper—as itself a "science." "In virtue of that necessity this pathway to science is itself *eo ipso* science ..." (*I*, §16; *PM*, p. 144). Actually the movement is necessary, because it is a dialectical one. For dialectic means the way that, within such a movement, one stage, the thesis, necessarily leads into another, the antithesis, and from thence goes over into the synthesis. We emphasized that the phenomenologist—starting from the movement of experience at a given stage, which necessarily leads, for him, to a specific result—perceives the character of the movement as a dialectic; he sees how, by negation of the sense-contents implicit in the contradictions, the transition is made from an old object to a "new" one (cf. *I*, §§7 and 14; *PM*, pp. 137, 142–43). Hence this dialectical movement presents itself to him as a progressive determination, which takes place "so and not otherwise," and is in this sense "necessary." Because this necessity prevails, and thus all the steps are "completely determined," they can be "presented" as such—which implies that, for this reason alone, this road does not have to be "an esoteric possession of a few individuals" (*P*, §13; *PM*, p. 76). It is only because of this exoteric character that the phenomenologist is able to fulfill the one role assigned to him, namely to persuade the contemporary natural consciousness, the reflection-philosophy of the understanding, that in virtue of its own inherent principle it could advance to science, if only it wanted to do so.

For our question about the phenomenologist's role, however, it is important to point out that the Preface, written only after completion of the work, does not see the ground for the "scientific character" of the Phenomenology in this category of necessity, but finds it in the movement of concepts or spiritual entities (or essentialities). In the Preface we are told (§34; *PM*, p. 95): "This movement of the spiritual entities constitutes the nature of scientific procedure in general." With express reference to the *Phenomenology of Spirit* it is further said that "the road which leads to the notion of knowledge becomes [through these entities] itself likewise a necessary and complete evolving process. This preparatory stage thus ceases to consist of casual philosophical reflections. . . ." This road—so the paragraph ends —"by the very movement of the notion itself, will compass the entire objective world of conscious life in its rational necessity." [1]

In Frankfurt, and then later in Jena, Hegel had already set forth, in various versions of his "Science of Logic," how the "pure thought-determinations, determinate concepts, spiritual entities". move by means of *the concept*. At the end of the *Phenomenology of Spirit* (p. 562; *PM*, p. 805) this movement of the determinate concepts, as the "organic . . . self-constituted process of these notions," is sharply distinguished from the manner in which the movement "of these moments" takes place in the Phenomenology of Spirit. The "further development" of the *pure* concept in logic "depends"—so it is there said—"solely on its pure characteristic nature." The manner in which the pure concept progresses through the determinacy of the concepts or pure essentialities has been specified by the Preface in many respects. In the element of pure thought, as realization of the concept, the pure essentialities organize themselves on the basis of the differences in their content into the "truth in the form of truth" (*P*, §37, and cf. §§5, 18; *PM*, pp. 97, 70–71, 80–81). This movement of the "speculative" is articulated in science proper by means of a "speculative presentation" (cf. *P*, §§58 ff., 62, 64, and 66 ff.; *PM*, pp. 116 ff., 121, 122, 123 ff.)

But how does the concept move the pure essentialities in the *Phenomenology of Spirit?* The final paragraphs of the Introduction have already told us that there the moments by no means appear as "pure and abstract," but as "shapes of consciousness." We also know already that in the Phenomenology the movement consists in the sublation of the distinction between knowledge, on the one hand, and on the other, the objectivity negative thereto, wherein all determinate shapes of consciousness are presented (*P*, §36; *PM*, p. 96). We have seen how negative objectivity is ultimately the standard and mode wherein other thought-determinations appear as "truth," which are valid for consciousness. The objectivity negative to knowledge is in its abstract constitution a "moment" or "spiritual entity." The fact that phenomenal knowledge distinguishes only unclearly, if at all, between this objectivity, *qua* form, and the presented object, *qua* content, is, as already explained, one of the features peculiar to the natural consciousness as phenomenal knowledge.

We have seen, indeed, how the distinction of "knowledge and truth" is sublated in each shape by phenomenal knowledge itself casting the truth so far valid for it as a "nothing" into the abyss, and turning to a new one; and how only the phenomenologist perceives in this a movement which, owing to its dialectical character, successively gathers the objects and the experiences obtained of them into a "system of experience." This would imply that only through the movement of the "experience" of phenomenal knowledge—made perspicuous through the observation of the phenomenologist—the movement of those pure essentialities takes place, constituting the nature of the scientific as such. If that were so, the Preface (§34; *PM*, p. 95) would not have extended the phenomenologist's role beyond that which constitutes, in the Introduction, the moment of "being *per se* or for us." But what does it mean then, when—as already quoted—it is said in the same paragraph that the road whereby the concept of knowledge is reached in the *Phenomenology* "by the very movement of the notion itself, will compass the entire objective world of conscious life in its rational necessity"? (See n. 1 above.)

The paragraph immediately following takes up the movement from the standpoint of "spirit." The spirit becomes an object to itself, in that it posits itself as "the element of . . . immediate existence" (*P*, §35; *PM*, p. 96). We explained earlier why—in accordance with the program already proposed in the *Differenzschrift*—the spirit must posit itself as an "appearance," in order, in this element, to again "construe" the understanding's distinction of knowledge and object into the identity of the absolute. In this sense the *Phenomenology of Spirit* and its presentation of phenomenal knowledge is itself an appearance of the absolute or of spirit. In the *Phenomenology*, the spirit becomes other to itself, in that it emerges in the mode of shapes of consciousness, containing in themselves the opposition of knowledge and truth, or of self and spiritual substance, and sublating this distinction in the manner depicted, in a history of experience concerned with the "simple" (the essentialities) prevailing in each case. From the spirit's point of view this represents a self-estrangement and return from this alienation back to itself. Does this movement of spirit embody the "movement of the notion [concept]" spoken of in the immediately preceding §34 (*PM*, p. 95) of the Preface? Since the movement of estrangement and return in fact embraces the "complete worldliness of consciousness in its necessity" (cf. n. 1 above), it seems legitimate to answer this question in the affirmative. According to §35 (*PM*, pp. 95–96) of the Preface, the "element of immediate existence" to which spirit has posited itself connotes the "science" of this road, and hence the *Phenomenology of Spirit*. This element is the "determination" through which this part of science is distinguished from the other parts: It is also through this determination that this science makes an "appearance"—in the manner described above (pp. 24 f.)—to which the "absolute" has reduced itself in order, at the level of phenomenal knowledge, to reveal the latter in its illusory character, and to instigate its abandonment of this illusion, so that it may liberate itself from the prevailing division (cf. above, p. 20).

That the spirit's "element of immediate existence" constitutes the "determination" of the *Phenomenology,* can also be understood as saying that this science carries itself out as the spirit which alienates itself, in that it analyzes its moments in the element of consciousness and distinguishes itself as objectivity, truth or "spiritual" substance from itself as the knowing self. The movement whereby this distinction is sublated constitutes—as is evident from the final chapter of the *Phenomenology*—the return from its alienation. The movement whereby the objectivity negative to knowledge—the truth, the thought-determinations, the essentialities—brings itself into unity with the self, is the "pathway" taken by the "science of this pathway," namely phenomenology. From this point of view the thinking of the phenomenologist would be nothing else but the mode in which the spirit realizes itself. The phenomenologist's "role" would then consist in the modes of a thinking realized by the spirit in the element of immediate existence. What sort of thinking is this, and what does it have to do with the "movement of the concept"?

In the Preface Hegel has failed to offer any specific definition of the phenomenologist's mode of thought. It would certainly be wrong to equate the latter with "conceptual" thinking, and to equate the presentation of the phenomenology with the "speculative" presentation,[2] and thus with science "proper," the science of logic; just as it would be wrong to wish to identify phenomenological thinking with the "merely ratiocinative knowledge" which the Preface sets apart from conceptual thought. Phenomenological thinking is certainly no "reflection" into the empty ego (*P, §59; PM,* p. 117).

Does Hegel perhaps regard the phenomenologist's thinking as "similar" to conceptual thought? The latter—according to the Preface (§54; *PM,* p. 113)—realizes itself by immersing itself in the "immanent self of the content," while simultaneously reverting into itself as the movement of pure "self-identity in otherness." Because the self has set aside its own fixity, like that of all the distinctions it makes (*P*, §33; *PM*, p. 95), it can lose itself in the subject matter, and "immerse" itself therein, and thereby become the "self-directing inner soul of the concrete content" (*P*, §53; *PM*, p. 111). In the *Logic*, by means of this pure thought, the meaning inherent in a given determination stirs into movement, and determines itself onward from thesis to antithesis, and from thence to the synthesis.

Can it be said that in the *Phenomenology* the "content" is consciousness as it maintains itself—especially in the key positions of the reflection-philosophy—still rooted in the distinction of knowledge and negative objectivity or truth? In that case the "presentation" would be the mode and manner in which phenomenological thinking immerses itself in this content; but since this content consists of the pure essentialities, the standards and ideas of consciousness—though as they are for consciousness, and not as they are in the pure thinking of logic—the effect of this immersion is to set the content of consciousness in motion. This means that such a movement of consciousness is ultimately first "set going" by this presentation. The presentation has the structure of a movement, and through it the pure essentialities begin to move for experience and execute the dialectical motion. This therefore derives from the movement of the presentation, as the "movement of the notion [concept]" which encompasses "the complete worldliness of consciousness in its necessity" (*P*, §34; *PM*, p. 95. See n. 1 above).

If this were so, the role of the phenomenologist—as the "being *per se* or for us" of the whole movement—would be essentially more significant than the account given in the Introduction would allow us to suppose. A clue which might support our interpretation is to be found on p. 556 of the *Phenomenology* (*PM*, p. 797 [amended]), where we read: "What we have contributed here is partly the *assembling* of the individual moments, each of which presents in its principle the life of the entire spirit, and partly the retention of the concept in the form of the

89

concept, whose content already disclosed itself in those moments and which already disclosed itself in the form of a *shape of consciousness*."

This assembling of the moments is performed by the presentation, and it is also the manner in which the concept is "retained" in the form of the concept. This yielded the content of the concept, as that whole history of experience whose result, in the form of the final shape of consciousness or spirit, is "spirit knowing itself in the shape of spirit, or *conceptual knowledge*" (*ibid.; PM,* p. 798 [amended]).

The only thing that matters to us here is that the presentation—which is to say, the phenomenologist—is thus the "initiator" of the movement carried out by phenomenal knowledge. We did indeed discover earlier that phenomenal knowledge is imbued with "despair" at all its given data, through the method of "self-realizing skepticism," only because the presentation "compels" it to this. We can now see more clearly that this compulsion lies in the "contribution" of "assembling," which first sets off the movement of experience and with it the movement of the entities.

We have now seen that it is only because the phenomenologist perceives the "necessity" in the movement of phenomenal knowledge, that he is able to fulfill the task of persuading the contemporary natural consciousness in an exoteric fashion. And only because his thinking has the movement-structure of the concept, is he able to instigate phenomenal knowledge, in virtue of its own principle, to determine itself further to absolute knowledge, and thereby to bring forth the concept of knowledge.

But if the phenomenologist is able to effect this assembling of the individual moments, as his "contribution," must he not then be already fully acquainted with them? But how is this to be reconciled with the other account of the Phenomenology, that it first "prepares" "the element of . . . knowledge" (*P,* §37; *PM,* p. 97), that in it "the element of science"—the pure concept—is first "produced" after a long journey (*P,* §27; *PM,* p. 88)? The solution to this apparent paradox lies in the "character" of the Phenomenology as an "appearance," already previously explained. We said that the Phenomenology is an "appearance" of the absolute, which reduces itself to this in order to be able to meet the shapes of "illusion," of untrue knowledge, on their own level, and to persuade them in so doing that the principle of a true knowledge is already implicit in them. If the absolute spirit posits itself in this fashion through its own "decree," this implies that it has already attained itself through actual history (cf. *PG*, p. 559; *PM*, p. 801), and now, in order to make itself perspicuous to the still fettered natural consciousness, has "released itself" to this appearance. The implication here is that it has in fact already taken on the "shape" of absolute knowledge, and as such is also capable of science proper, but that, precisely so that it may fulfill these tasks, it nonetheless "behaves" toward phenomenal knowledge as if it had not yet produced the concept of knowledge.

Phenomenological thinking has this hybrid shape, that although it is already absolute, it presents itself phenomenologically—that in accordance with §9 of the Introduction (*PM*, p. 139) it does not seek to behave absolutely, as a relating of science to phenomenal knowledge, but rather as an appearance which liberates itself, together with phenomenal knowledge, from the illusion of untruth. Precisely because of this hybrid nature, the phenomenologist can be the "guide," on the one hand, for phenomenal knowledge, and yet remain, on the other hand, at the latter's level and bring forth the concept of knowledge together with it.

Let us bring these accounts of the phenomenologist's role together, and then see whether we can also confirm them from the way in which the phenomenologist actually behaves in the expositions of the text.

The phenomenologist—so we found—is in the *first* place he who "takes" phenomenal knowledge "along" on the road. *Secondly*, he is the initiator of the movement of the history of experience, and hence also that of the dialectical history of experience. *Thirdly*, by means of his superior knowledge, the phenomenologist surveys the dialectical movement of experience and the category of necessity underlying it, which makes possible the exoteric presentation, and hence the "justification" vis-à-vis natural consciousness. *Fourthly,* as a result of the foregoing history of experience, there arises for the phenomenologist the synthesis positively apprehended as principle. *Fifthly,* he can act as a "guide" for phenomenal knowledge.

If we attend to the "expositions," which mostly precede the presentation of any given history of the experience of phenomenal knowledge, or are often inserted within the presentation of a given shape, we are able to observe the following: Before phenomenal knowledge itself enters into the examination, the phenomenologist shows that, and how, a "principle" has arisen for him out of the preceding dialectical movement of experience. He thereby reveals the nature of the "transition" from the preceding object to the "new one."

This is again to be seen very clearly in the first three paragraphs of the chapter on perception. We have already explained briefly above (pp. 80 f.) that, for Hegel, the dialectical movement which sense-certainty must perform in regard to its object, leads to a result. Being, the principle of sense-certainty, is indeed contained in this result, but as a principle which is transformed by the negating movement into a universal. "Being, however, is a universal by its having in it mediation or negation" (*PG,* p. 90; *PM,* p. 164). The transition to the principle of the universal therefore comes about automatically, if the negation presented by the experience of sense-certainty is viewed, not as destruction, but as a transformation or "sublation" having the "true twofold meaning" of negating and preserving (*ibid.; PM,* pp. 163–64). But only the philosopher is in a position to take this view.

The next thing he does is again to dissect this principle critically; he shows in anticipation how the new standard, the new abstract structure, develops in concrete modes of apprehension which are antithetically opposed. In the case of perception this takes place as follows: as said, the new principle was the universal as "immediacy," containing in itself negation, difference, or "manifoldness." Now the abstract structure of its content is not given as such to consciousness in its earlier stages, but is immediately one, for the latter, with the content or object

THE ROLE OF THE PHENOMENOLOGIST

given to it, since this object ranks for it as the "essence" (cf. *PG,* p. 89; *PM,* p. 162). How does the principle of perception appear in this object for the philosopher? The object has the structure of the universal, i.e., it is immediate or simple and simultaneously differentiated or manifold within itself. The object therefore ranks to the perceiving consciousness as "the thing with many properties" (*PG,* p. 90; *PM,* p. 163). To the philosopher, however, it is now clear that the principle harbors an opposition within it, namely, that of immediacy and mediation, simplicity and difference. This opposition must again be present in concrete form in the object of consciousness and in the modes of apprehending it. In fact, on pp. 90–92 of the chapter (*PM,* pp. 163–65), the philosopher develops the opposing aspects of the thing, and the opposing modes of perceptual apprehension, from the moments of the principle: that of negation or difference, and immediacy, and that of the unity of both, the immediacy which has negation in itself. Corresponding to the first moment is a mode of apprehension which puts excluding difference in the foreground, whether it be the mutual exclusion of different properties, or that of things taken as simple or "one." The mode corresponding to the second moment is that of indifference, of the existence of adjacent properties which do not mutually "affect" one another—a mode which therefore posits the thing as a mere "also," a collection of independent properties viewed as materials. The unity of both moments seems to present the view that the properties are indeed mutually exclusive, but belong to different things, whereas within their thing, viewed as "medium of subsistence," they are indifferent to each other. But with this difference, or these "in-so-far" properties—insofar as they belong to a thing they do not exclude each other, and do so only insofar as they belong to different things—perception fails to get the matter right. The philosopher can foresee this, because he grasps that in the principle of perception no synthesis of immediacy, or reference-to-self, and negation, or reference-to-another, has yet been attained. In fact, in its examination of the different modes of apprehension, perception is constantly driven to and fro between the moments of being-for-self and being-for-other.

It is therefore possible for the philosopher to foresee the contradiction which will finally drive perception into discerning the untruth of its standard, and to anticipate that a new principle must result from this, representing at least a preliminary solution of the contradiction in question. He might thus already anticipate the abstract form of this principle. But the principle will at the same time be a standard for phenomenal knowledge, and proceed from this experience. So the philosopher not only has to relate his anticipatory reflections to phenomenal knowledge, but must also launch the latter on the road of experience. This is the manner in which the presentation "takes" phenomenal knowledge "along with it," and in so doing compels it to self-examination, eliciting despair in it by the method of self-realizing skepticism. By this very encounter with the critique demonstrated by the phenomenologist, phenomenal knowledge itself will also be made to adopt a critical attitude. It is only by "immersing" himself in the "content" of consciousness through the presentation that the phenomenologist evokes this movement, whose dialectical nature he had discerned in the "necessity" of its phases. Not only is the presentation of phenomenal knowledge "exoteric" on that account; the same is true of its preceding exposition. Above all, however, the exposition is the "guide" for the history of experience of phenomenal knowledge. If the latter—still as natural consciousness—often knows its standard only vaguely, and often "professes" other standards than those which actually guide it, it still always follows precisely the standard of the phenomenologist, at the outset of the presentation of any given shape, and within its projected phases.

In order to understand this underlying Idea of the Phenomenology, the following should also be noted: we saw that the "justification," which the Phenomenology of Spirit has to provide, consists above all in having to make its "standpoint" "intelligible" to the consciousness of Hegel's own day, so as to provoke the latter into "further educating" itself by joining Hegel on the road to science and transforming itself into an absolute knowledge which can enter into the science of the absolute. But in order to reach this goal, Phenomenology must allow the contemporary understanding a number of concessions, whose nature we have still to depict in detail.

As we saw, the contemporary natural consciousness is to become apprised of its past substance. For this very reason the movement of the Phenomenology does not first begin at the state of the history of education in which the contemporary consciousness already finds itself, but goes back, rather, to the cultural positions which took shape at the outset of the history of Western thought. Purpus has shown convincingly that, and how, the entire history of experience constituting Section A—to be discussed by way of example in what follows—contains positions which originally took form in Greek philosophy.[3] Section B then traces the development from the beginnings of the Roman world—which lay for Hegel in the struggle for recognition and in the relationship of lordship and bondage emerging from it— up to the Christianity of the Middle Ages, whose nature Hegel expounds in the principle of the "unhappy consciousness." The development beginning with Section C comprises the modern formation of the natural consciousness. This connection between the Phenomenology and the history of philosophy can be confirmed from Hegel's own descriptions. Nevertheless—as can be clearly seen in Chapter III of Section A—he has elucidated the development taking place, for example, in Greek philosophy by means of determinations, like that of "force," which are reminiscent of Leibniz, or, like the dualism of appearance and supersensory world, recall the philosophy of Kant. The first reason for this is that Hegel, as we have seen, envisaged the task of the Phenomenology as consisting in a "justification" directed to the *contemporary* natural consciousness; precisely because it has to make the element of science "comprehensible," it must be presented in a language and mode of thought accessible to that consciousness. For this very reason the entire presentation derives as such from the principle on which modern philosophy is founded, the principle of self-consciousness. From thence the development of Greek philosophy—to which the conception of "consciousness" was quite unknown—can be genetically depicted as a process leading from consciousness to self-consciousness. Since self-consciousness has shown itself, for Hegel, as the "concept," the succession of shapes becomes a "conceived" history (cf. *PG*, p. 564; *PM*, p. 807), depending not at all on the contingent sequence of occurrence, but on the order required by the concept of knowledge. The necessity of the successive stages required by the concept of knowledge is connected, indeed, with the experience which consciousness has with its ideas of knowledge—or determinations of the concept, as the phenomenologist sees them. For it is the negative result of any given experience which the phenomenologist recognizes as "determinate nothing," and hence positively as the new shape. This connection with the experience of consciousness does not, however, imply that we are dealing here with a "universal history"; the concern is rather with a "genesis" of the concept of knowledge. For this very reason, the historical element in which the shapes make their appearance is far less important than the conceptual element. For an understanding of the Phenomenology, the only thing really of decisive importance is the way in which the essentialities or categorial determinations belonging to the self, or concept, become organized into a system, precisely through the experience that is had of them. To understand the Phenomenology, attention is needed, therefore, not so much to the historical aspect of the genesis—with which one can easily become acquainted in Hegel's Lectures on History—but rather to the aspect of categorial development which is so very much more difficult to understand, and not least because it has been carried through only in very cryptic fashion by Hegel himself.

NOTES

1. "This movement of the pure entities constitutes the nature of what is scientific. . . . The way in which the Concept of knowledge is reached thus also becomes a necessary and complete becoming. Hence this preparation ceases to be a fortuitous bit of philosophizing. . . . Rather this

THE ROLE OF THE PHENOMENOLOGIST

way will encompass, by virtue of the movement of the Concept, the complete worldliness of consciousness in its necessity" (*K*, p. 410).

2. On the problems of the speculative presentation, cf. my *Absolute Reflexion und Sprache*, Frankfurt 1967; in English, under the title "Reason and Language," in my *Reason and World*, The Hague 1971.

3. W. Purpus, *Zur Dialektik des Bewusstseins nach Hegel*, Berlin 1908.

VII

The Idea of the Phenomenology of Spirit and Its Significance for the Understanding of Post-Hegelian Philosophy

Now WHERE, in summary, does the idea of the *Phenomenology of Spirit* lie, as we have attempted to define it? It lies in the principle of self-consciousness. It is this that can supply the "justification" which makes up this "preparatory" and "introductory" science—a justification in the twofold sense we have pointed out: on the one hand as a demonstration of the necessary emergence of a scientific consciousness, that of absolute knowledge, and on the other, as a vindication in the sense that even the unscientific consciousness of Hegel's own day will be thereby convinced that it, too, could attain to this absolute knowledge, if only it would embark on the road which the exposition has pointed out. The possibility of such a justification proved to be grounded in the principle, and thus in the conceptual nature of self-consciousness, because the latter, *qua* logical form, performs a movement of reflection which is not merely static—like the Kantian transcendental apperception—but proceeds historically, in dialectical steps, along the "road of experience," and is able, through its relation to the differing forms of objectivity, to fill itself with content, and so can fashion itself, "for itself," into a universal self-consciousness. Since self-consciousness, *qua* principle, is conceptual in nature, it is able increasingly to overcome the opposition between knowledge and objectivity implicit in its shape at any point, to "purify" itself from all the givenness and foreign-

98

ness in this objectivity, and to become more and more aware of the identity of this being with its own thought. Self-consciousness can be true, scientific, absolute knowledge. It has then liberated itself from all constraints of the objectivity confronting it, in the sense that it knows the latter's rationality to be identical with "its own" reason, and has apprehended the spirit at work therein to be "its own." In nature, in the ideas constituting its own situation, in the institutions and customs of its people, and ultimately in all determinations of otherness, it perceives the discernible movement of thought-determinations which as such are all modes of a "self" no longer to be regarded as an empty solipsistic ego, but as a fully understood, "universal," rational self-consciousness, and thus as the self-conceiving concept. This conceiving, enlarged into true knowledge, which is able, while remaining at home with itself in otherness, to bring to presentation the system of these thought-determinations, namely truth, has overcome division and in light of truth has again found the true, and found itself in the true. Through this consciously performed reconciliation of everything spiritual with its own spirit, it has achieved "liberation" from all natural constraints—a liberation effected solely by means of, and on the basis of, this truth. This principle of self-consciousness, implanted in every man as such, contains, therefore, the promise of a "rational" humanity that can consciously come to partake of the truth. In that self-consciousness can learn, in all fields of existence, to rediscover the thought-determinations belonging to the presented system as "its own," "the truth" can make it free. This liberation should not be confused with the sense of freedom later developed by Hegel in the philosophy of history. There the *telos* of an eschatologically conceived history is determined to freedom through the consciousness of progress, a freedom that mankind can also secure without coming to partake of truth, in the sense that this happens in the final shape of spirit, namely absolute knowledge, in the Phenomenology of Spirit.

Another very important "message" of the Phenomenology of Spirit, which we have elicited from its developed "Idea," is that this liberation cannot take place without guidance and assistance from the philosopher. Without this, the natural unscientific consciousness would remain at the cultural stage of "division of life." It may well have an uneasy sense of the need to overcome this division, but the philosopher has first to persuade it that it is itself capable of taking the road to scientific consciousness. Only when the phenomenologist undertakes to present the whole road genetically; only when he immerses himself in the essentialities presaging that road, and initiates and maintains their movement, whose course runs quite definitely in the direction of absolute knowledge; only when by subjectivity and categorial reflection he imparts and preserves movement in the cultural and historical substance of the various shapes of consciousness— then only, as we have seen, can the necessity be manifested of arriving at that ultimate shape of the spirit, absolute knowledge. It is only because the phenomenologist is able, in this fashion, to persuade the unscientific consciousness, that the complete unfolding of the latter's inherent principle of self-consciousness can become possible. The contribution of philosophy is not therefore confined to being a "propaedeutic." It does not fulfill its task by merely presenting the cultural history of mankind, or by teaching the natural consciousness to adopt a "critical attitude." On the contrary, the philosopher must first himself have carried out the principle of self-consciousness dialectically, before the latent reason can come to fruition. Only if the philosopher's role in the Phenomenology is viewed in all its significance, can it be said that with this "Idea" of the Phenomenology we are confronted with the final shape of traditional, and hence also of modern, metaphysics: since its inception among the Greeks, metaphysics has proceeded, first on the assumption that mankind is potentially "rational," can come to participate in truth, and thereby attain freedom, and secondly on the belief that philosophy has a decisive role to play in this.

Let us ask in conclusion, what significance the "Idea" of the Phenomenology of Spirit, as we have now expounded it, can have for an understanding of the development of philosophy from Hegel to the present day. In the context of this inquiry we shall expressly leave out of consideration whether, and how, Hegel, in the system he evolved after 1807, may have altered or even thrown doubt upon the meaning and significance of this Idea.[1] Nor are we inquiring into the history of the "influence" of this Idea; we merely wish to point out briefly how it can assist in an understanding of the development that followed.

We must make it clear that the principle of self-consciousness has by no means developed in accordance with this Idea. Not merely has it realized itself without the assistance of philosophy —the "potential" inherent in the conceptual nature of self-consciousness has also by no means evolved in the direction to which Hegel pointed it in the *Phenomenology*. It has not become a scientific consciousness, seeing it as its sole task to know everything as the spirit that is akin to its own spirit. It has not so liberated itself through truth as to have sought in every field the thought-determinations of the universal self, and to have found itself again therein. The "need" that Hegel had defined, at the time of his first publication (1801), as the "need of philosophy," the need to find a way out from the "division" of life (*Differenzschrift, Werke,* I, p. 172), was certainly no longer the need of philosophy in the post-Hegelian era. Whereas even in Hegel's day, "so-called commonsense" may have had no taste for this (cf. *Werke,* I, p. 183)—in the period that followed no such need could have been present, on the non-philosophical plane, in face of the growing power of the natural sciences and the effects of the industrial revolution. Nor, indeed, did post-Hegelian philosophy betray any sort of further "need" to clamber up the "ladder" to "science" in order to be able to approach it. This decline of speculation must already have been sensed by Hegel shortly before his death, when at the end of the second Preface to the *Science of Logic* he wrote of his doubt "whether the noisy clamour of current affairs and the deafening chatter of a conceit which prides itself on confining itself to such matters leave any room for participation in the passionless calm of a knowledge which is in the element of pure thought alone" (*WL,* I, p. 22; *HSL,* p. 42).

Leaving aside the positions of Hegelianism and Neo-Kantianism, the development of philosophy has essentially taken the course of transforming the principle of self-consciousness from its logical form into an anthropological one (Feuerbach), or of employing its movement-structure, reflection, simply as a critical instrument directed to the socio-economic facts of the period, as material for criticism. This thought metamorphosed into socio-critical reflection took over its *telos,* the consciousness of freedom, from the Hegelian philosophy of history and not from the *Phenomenology of Spirit.* The movement-pattern of this critical thinking has its essential source in the Cartesian principle of self-consciousness: the movement of reflection relates to itself and its mode of cognition, and also at the same time to the sphere of objectivity, as that which is known by this cognition. It also has its root in the logico-dialectical version of this principle, in that the sphere of objectivity is apprehended in opposing determinations, which then have to be construed into identity. This reflection, however, unlike that of Hegel, is still directed to the "realm of the empirical." And since it has forsaken any kind of "system," it also renounces the standard of a truth, which for Hegel had consisted in the completeness of the dialectically interrelated thought-determinations. That this critical reflection of the Young Hegelians (such as Ruge and Bauer) is founded on the principle of self-consciousness, is in no need of further proof. We may leave open here the question whether, and in what sense, the Marxian project for a new kind of human rationality—as the rationality of a concrete, sensuously natural and no longer alienated individual —and that of the society transformed by these new men, still rests upon the principle of self-consciousness. We may also leave aside the further question whether this anti-idealist type of rationality, even in the negation of its principles (such as that of identity), still remains a part of the traditional *logos* and *telos* philosophy. It may likewise be left undecided whether the notion of a "revolutionary practice" is still founded upon the concept of subjectivity. It is nevertheless certain that, despite its pursuit of materialistic concreteness, the Marxian critique of ideology and science of historical economics is a "movement of reflection" which, notwithstanding its altered dialectical structure—when compared with that of Hegel—has its essential origin in the principle of self-consciousness. Thought which is aware of itself and its medium, and is turned, in this self-relation, upon the economic and historical aspects of society, attempts, by unfolding the contradictions inherent therein, to arrive at an insight into historico-social reality. And just as with this critical reflection of Marx, so also with the method of the "critical theory," which conceives itself to be a transformation of Marxism; this, too, can be derived from the principle of self-consciousness, since it relies upon the "power of self-reflection." [2]

If it be granted that in the "Idea" of the *Phenomenology of Spirit* here elaborated this principle has been unfolded with a maximum of coherence, it should be possible to use it as a "standard" for estimating how far, despite all their diversity, these various post-Hegelian developments have remained faithful to its inherent principle, or to what extent they depart from it. But the "Idea" of the *Phenomenology of Spirit* can also be regarded as a "standard" in a sense decidedly the "reverse" of this. Within certain trends of contemporary philosophy characteristics have developed which can be construed as "opposites" to this Idea. In this sense, at any rate, it can be viewed as a "point of orientation" for all attempts, explicit or implicit, at an "overcoming of subjectivity," in which, positively regarded, the road to a wholly different conception of thinking may lie. We shall show in what follows how a different view of the nature of man, of the sphere of "objectivity," of the relation of each to the other, of the nature of truth and of the role of the philosopher, can be discerned in a manner opposed to this Idea. And here the position worked out by Heidegger may serve us as an example of such opposition in its most radical form.

1. In the *Lebensphilosophie* typified especially by Nietzsche and Dilthey, the definition of man's nature as reason and spirit has already become problematic, and with this the view of the self derived from the principle of self-consciousness, whether in its Cartesian or its transcendental and absolute form. But in

present-day thought the "crisis of reason" (Ortega y Gasset) has grown sharper still. At the very moment when man, in the certainty of his increasing knowledge, has begun to set forth fully his claim to dominance over nature and his fellow men by the means of modern technology, the empirical sciences of psychology, psychiatry, psychoanalysis, and biology have revealed to him the limits of a "rationality" which claims to be completely certain and in control of itself, and able to govern both itself and everything else. Whether influenced by this or not, philosophy has attempted in various ways to demonstrate that the question of man's nature cannot be adequately worked out under the guidance of the traditional concept of reason and the subject. The anthropological school, which attempted to show that thinking is only one of the capacities included in a total and concrete view of human nature, has failed, however, to provide a "foundation" for this. Edmund Husserl's attempt at a radicalization and completion of Cartesianism and transcendental philosophy —which in itself must be regarded as a reversion to the principle of self-consciousness and even to an idealistic point of view— contains, especially in its later development, motives which have driven the question of man's nature onto a road opposite to that of the "Idea" of the Phenomenology. Husserl's demand for the "self-givenness" of everything, which also implies the mode of man's self-givenness, like his insight into the grounding-power of "original" experiences, has contributed to Heidegger's taking as his theme the "facticity" of human existence by means of an analysis of *Dasein* which no longer sets out from "consciousness," but tries to discover the particular modes of Being of that which factually exists. The theme is no longer the *cogitare* unfolded into absolute reflection, the self-certain subject as performer of acts, but rather the Being of the individual being, who by virtue of his "understanding of Being" relates—within the range of possibilities of his environment and historical horizon— to his own Being, to the Being of others, and to the Being of things. Heidegger's account of the "care-structure" of *Existenz*, and more particularly the temporal analysis of "finitude," must be regarded as opposed to the principle of self-consciousness.[3]

Heidegger's analyses of *Dasein* do nothing, indeed, to "refute" the principle, as consummated in the "Idea" of the Phenomenology. But in a fundamental fashion they have given to man the possibility of understanding himself in a way that is specifically "opposed" to that view. It should be noted that Heidegger's later account of man's essence, which abandons all traditional modes of thought, represents a still more radical opposition to the "Idea" in question. A *Dasein* "eventuated" from Being is assuredly no self-certain founding-and-grounding subject, and certainly not one which exists as self-conceiving concept. It can only harken to the claim of the event and conform to it.

2. As we have seen, it is part of the "Idea" of the Phenomenology of Spirit that the self is able to rediscover itself in all fields of objectivity and in the categories operative there. The natural sciences of our own day have raised the question—admittedly only on an empirical basis—whether "nature" and its laws are altogether open to our view. The social sciences, primarily through an analysis of the history of this century, and of its political, social, and institutional disintegration, have likewise sown doubt concerning the existence of a rationally objective spirit, a moral substance of peoples or even of mankind, in which the individual could again discover himself. While in the nineteenth century, philosophy, in the persons of Feuerbach, Marx, Kierkegaard, and Nietzsche, had already bitterly attacked the view that the world is rational, in contemporary philosophy there has been a thoroughgoing attempt to show that, and how, the world is constituted in an "original" manner opposite to that of the Hegelian "concept in itself." In his later philosophy Husserl defined the "life-world" of prescientific experience as the field or horizon within which this experience operates in an immediately intuitive fashion. The retreat from the world determined and set forth by the "objectivism" of the sciences to this "natural" world underlying it, must be seen as a position specifically opposed to the definition of objectivity inherent in the principle of self-consciousness and hence in the "Idea" of the Phenomenology of Spirit. This life-world of everyday commonplaces, and of practice, is ruled by no traditionally-

conceived categories of the self, in which it could consciously re-discover itself. The experience of such a life-world operates there in the certainty of faith, trusting to its "typic" and anticipating its horizons in a pre-predicative fashion. Though this life-world, for Husserl, was still a "formation," since it owed its origin to the experiential achievements of the community of subjects, the "passive" constitution of the life-world of such life-worldly experiences must nonetheless be regarded as directly opposed to the standpoint of absolute knowledge. But here too we find a far more radical opposition in Heidegger's analyses of *Dasein,* and especially in his late philosophy. The worldhood of being-in-the world, of the environmental ambiency, of the "wherein" of a meaningful totality of reference, in which *Dasein* constantly "signifies" itself in careful circumspection, betokens transcendence in the sense of a vague understanding of Being, and not in that of a subjectivity which embraces objectivity. But the most ex-treme opposition to the account of objectivity implicit in the "Idea" of the *Phenomenology* is to be found in Heidegger's later view of the world as a realm—occurring first, admittedly, in an "other beginning," and "suddenly" at that—which simply cannot become present to founding-and-grounding thought—let alone to a concept conceiving itself in a field of categories. The particular "regions" of world into which, for Heidegger, human habitation originally grounds itself can become present only to a "poietic" experience. World, so regarded, as an utterly opaque realm which has ever determined and surpassed man's nature, would then have to be the proper dimension from whence the other "principle" opposed to the principle of self-consciousness would have to be derived.

3. The opposition to the relationship of thought and Being, as tradition has conceived it since Parmenides' time, and as it has developed in the modern era, in the principle of self-consciousness of Kant's transcendental logic, and then subse-quently in German Idealism as the idea of an "identity," finds likewise its most radical expression in the late philosophy of Heidegger. What typifies this "relationship" for Heidegger is not the consciousness, inherent in absolute knowledge, of a synthesis,

an identity, "resulting" from the non-identity of knowledge and objectivity, but rather the experience of a "belonging" to the "event" by a harkening and conforming to "mission" (*Geschick*). Here there is no "liberation" attained by the "self's re-cognition of itself in the thought-determinations operative in every field; instead, a poietic *Dasein* has experienced "being conditioned" and determinacy as its nature, and found the meaning of its existence in this true belonging to the event.

4. The decisive opposition to the "Idea" of the Phenomenology here elaborated is to be seen, however, in the view of the nature of "truth" underlying all the basic definitions of Heidegger's later philosophy. The "truth" to which the introductory and preparatory science of phenomenology leads, in the final shape of absolute knowledge, consists in the dialectically assembled system of thought-determinations. This totally manifest truth is the last and most extreme expression of the principle of total lucidity inherent in *logos* and *nous*. Heidegger views the nature of truth as a process in which "hiddenness"—lethe—so passes, within a realm of clearing—aletheia—into "disclosure," as to permeate the latter further in various ways. This view of the "essence of an original truth" is his sharpest "weapon" against the principle of subjectivity. If what is shown to knowledge or conceiving is merely a side of Being permeated by hiddenness, or actually "withdrawing" itself from truth proper, we then have a thought running radically counter to the possibility that the self-conceiving concept, the self evolving toward true knowledge, should be able to rediscover itself in the complete movement of thought-determinations, *qua* systematic truth.[4]

5. The role which Heidegger assigned to the philosopher in the unfolding of this "truth," and of the relationships of event, Being, world, and *Dasein* thought out from it, is most radically opposed, within the development of contemporary philosophy, to the role played by the phenomenologist in the *Phenomenology of Spirit*. The "thinker" is not required, by immersing himself in the concept, to inaugurate the further dialectical determination of the latter, to keep this in motion, and

to present it as it moves; he simply has to listen to the claim addressed to him and articulate it in language. He has no need to provide any "justification" of science proper, in the twofold sense described, for he is simply not concerned to bring forth a concept of science, or to induce the contemporary consciousness to advance toward an exoterically conceived science. On the contrary, the "thinker" sees it as his task, in the face of all contemporary tendencies, to prepare the possibility of an "other beginning."

The Idea of the Phenomenology of Spirit has thus proved to be a standard by which to assess the development of post-Hegelian thought, by reference both to the further validity of the principle of subjectivity, and also to the attempt at overcoming it.

NOTES

1. Cf. on this point H. F. Fulda, *Das Problem* . . . , who defends the necessity of the *Phenomenology* even from the standpoint of the later system; see especially pp. 289, 299, and 301.

2. Cf. J. Habermas, *Technik und Wissenschaft als "Ideologie,"* Frankfurt 1968, p. 164. We are not unaware here that Habermas wishes to view reflection materialistically, as bound up with the "natural history of the human race." For all that, his notion that reason has an interest in maturity, which finds expression in self-reflection, and which, as Habermas puts it, is "theoretically certain" or can "be discerned a priori" (*op. cit.*, p. 163), remains oriented toward Hegel's perception of the power of self-consciousness to liberate itself from all the ties of "naturalness."

3. For this and what follows, cf. the author's *Heidegger und die Tradition,* Stuttgart 1961; on the opposition between Hegel and Heidegger, see especially pp. 52 ff., 93 ff., 110 ff. (English version in *Heidegger and the Tradition,* Evanston 1971, pp. 43 ff., 85 ff., 102 ff.).

4. Cf. here the author's *Vernunft und Welt,* The Hague 1970, pp. 85 ff., 101 ff. (English version in *Reason and World,* The Hague 1971, pp. 82 ff., 100 ff.).

Index

Order, xxi
Ortega y Gasset, J., 104
Otherness, xix, 38, 44, 47

Parmenides, 106
"*Per se*," 9, 69, 72 ff.
Perception, xix, 67, 69, 71 f., 80 f.,
  92 f.
Philosophy, need for, 15 f., 21, 43, 101
Plato, 66
Pöggeler, O., x, xiv, xv, xvi, 77
Presentation, xxii, 1, 13, 15, 21 ff., 27,
  44, 63 f., 70, 89 f., 94
Principle, 16, 22, 92 f.
  of science, 34
  of self-consciousness, 2, 22, 35, 75 f.,
  98 f., 102
Propaedeutic, ix, 22, 31, 100
Purpus, W., 95, 97

Realphilosophie, xi
Reason, 23, 34, 42 f., 99
  crisis of, 104
Reflection, xviii, 2, 36 ff., 42 ff., 103
  culture, 42
  philosophy of, 2, 21 f., 36, 42, 89
Religion, xi, xxi, 55 f.
Riedel, M., 76
Rosenkranz, K., xiii
Ruge, A., 102

Schelling, F. W. J., xv, xvii f., 20, 37,
  43, 45
Schmitz, H., 5
Science, xxi, 1, 18 f., 21 ff., 33 ff., 56, 84
  education to, 21, 28
  of experience, x, 1, 53, 62
  road to, 23, 84
Self, xx, 16, 44, 55
  certainty of, 34 ff., 55

-consciousness, xix, xxi, 2, 10, 35 f.,
  45, 75 f., 98 ff.
-examination, 69 ff., 79
-intuition, xviii
-knowledge, 43
  reflection into, 48, 103
-sameness, 71 f.
Shape, 3, 5 f., 13, 25 f., 60 f., 73, 81 f.,
  86, 90 f., 96
Skepticism, 51 f., 76, 90, 94
Spinoza, B., 44 f., 48
Spirit, 29, 32, 54 ff., 87, 90
  absolute, xxi, 30, 54 f., 59 f.
Standard, 66 f., 70 f., 73, 103
Subject, 2, 44, 46, 48
-object, xix, xxi f., 10, 36, 38, 42
Subjectivity, xxi, 11, 16, 20, 46, 67
  overcoming of, 103
Sublation, 46, 48
Substance, x, xxii f., 4, 32, 44 ff., 54
System, ix f., xii, xxiii, 10, 60, 83

Telos, xxii f., 28, 33, 35, 82, 99, 102
Thing, 66, 69 ff., 80, 93
Thinking, xix, xxii, 4, 16, 19, 35, 45,
  58, 88, 91, 107
Thought-determination, 4, 10 f., 18,
  68 f., 73
Transcendental
  apperception, xix ff., 8, 49, 52, 98
  philosophy, x, 2
Truth, 7 f., 40, 49, 66 ff., 73, 85 f.,
  99, 107

Understanding, xix, xxii, 17 ff., 22,
  43, 47
Universal, 17, 81, 92 f.

World, 106
  history, xi, 32 f., 40, 60